PEACE COMES DROPPING SLOW

PEACE COMES DROPPING SLOW

CHRISTOPHER RUSH

THE RAMSAY HEAD PRESS EDINBURGH

First published in 1983 by
The Ramsay Head Press
15 Gloucester Place
Edinburgh EH3 6EE

Reprinted 1990

Printed in Scotland by
W. M. Bett Ltd, Tillicoultry

The publisher acknowledges the
financial assistance of the
Scottish Arts Council in the
publication of this volume.

Contents

Me and My St Monans

ST MONANS bore me.

A salt-splashed cradle with a golden fringe.

And even now, it is that same cradle that rocks me nightly towards my grave.

St Monan is supposed to have come to Fife in the ninth century in the company of Adrian and his monkish followers. Knowing no worse weapon than the Viking axe, beneath which he fell, he nonetheless prophesied, I am told, that at the time of the end of the world strange lights would be shot up into space; not as candles to a dying god, but as eyes that would be witnesses to the final holocaust.

As I look before and after, from the year nineteen hundred and eighty two, the saint's martyrdom seems as close to me now as the world's end and my own quiet beginning.

I am blessed, or cursed, with one of those memories like Wordsworth's or Hardy's, that allows me to reach far down the well-shaft of my years and draw up images and experiences by the bucketful. I can still recall the waiting-room-green bars of my cot (from the inside) and my mother's pale face peeping through. It was war-time and my father was in the Navy. By the time I had learned to walk the war was over, but its depressive fall-out lasted well into my childhood – ration coupons and margarine, which I accepted naturally without the slightest feelings of gloom; it was part of life. Luxuries were not. And so the peace-time plane that was forced to jettison its crates of groceries above the town's natural swimming pond must have been looked upon by even adult villagers as one of the most benign of great silver birds.

My grandmother told me the story. In my imagination the village headmaster became a Pied Piper of Hamlin in reverse. He opened up the great gloomy cave of the primary school and allowed the children to burst forth like an underground river, making madly for the sea. Not Spanish doubloons and pieces-of-eight were plucked up by the score, but Chivers jellies and tins of fruit and packets of peanuts – a treasure-trove indeed! Such manna falls seldom from some people's skies, and into the lives of most folk never at all.

1

Our house was on a hill.

I remember my pram running down it out of control one frosty winter's night – perhaps my mother had slipped on the icy road – and seeing my right hand scoring itself against the prickly wall of the house. A dark, crimson curtain-fall of velvet over my fingers; much adult concern. Yet no memory of pain. Instead, what I remember most vividly of all is the sheer richness of the eighteen-carat gold moon that night and the precious nearness of the stars. How I wondered what they were.

Another pram memory rekindles for me a glowing journey, a journey for snowdrops. Balcaskie wood was a great green gothic cathedral. Its nave was a mile-long footpath, soft with a prayer-carpet of moss and vaulted over by the interlocking boughs of elms and oaks. Along this path, known locally as 'The Bishop's Walk', my mother wheeled me for snowdrops from the estate. They were presented to me by a green-caped girl, now a white-haired lady, but whose glad young smile lights up my remembering.

Alas, 'The Bishop's Walk', which I Lord-Byroned my way along in my early teens, is no more. The landowner wanted a view of the sea. I heard a worker say that when they were tearing up trees by the roots, strange shoals of skulls were fished up in the great fibrous nets. If so, I am sure they were screaming ones! The conservational damage done to the woods by the Fife lairds and farmers is incalculable – and all in the name of the almighty pound. It is said that when James IV was building the Scottish Navy he had all the woods in Fife cut down just to build one colossal vessel. That was a high kind of price, even to make possible sea-captains like the legendary Sir Andrew Wood of Largo. Still, the defence of Scotland was a noble end. Nowadays they tear up trees and place caravans on the desolation. Primitive peoples used to worship trees because of the spirits which they believed resided in them. If their beliefs have any foundation in truth, I know some Fife farmers who must go haunted to their graves. Their greed for gold has caused one possible derivation of the name 'Fife' (a Danish word meaning 'the wooded country') to become less appropriate in our own time. Some folk can see beauty in nothing but a pound note.

Our landlady was an old lady called Epp, whom I remember well, though she died before I was three. She was my earliest human contact with the Victorian age, for she was in her eighties then. Indeed, it is remarkable how long are the joints that dovetail one era to another, and how incongruous the human inter-penetrations that sometimes result. As an example of this, I knew a Cellardyke man who had talked with a lady who had been at the battle of Trafalgar! The lady was his great-grandmother and her father had been press-ganged. She was born at sea during the bombardment of Copenhagen in 1801, and was at Trafalgar at the age of four-and-a-half, with her father, who was by then a bosun gunner on board the *Victory*. I have turned this into one of my stories, *Earth's Highest Station*. Or take a literary example. When the poet Crabbe died in 1832 he was still an ardent admirer of the poetry of Pope. Yet Wordsworth had composed all his best poetry by then, Keats, Byron and Shelley were dead and doing well, and Tennyson had already begun to write.

In fact it was Epp who first quoted Tennyson to me: *The Charge of the Light Brigade*. Throned on her massive moss-green velvet armchair, all curves and buttons, she would sit there in a black waterfall of lace, her skirts spilling over the floor, and thunder out the words. In retrospect I feel like a tiny Mr Tennyson or Gladstone in reverse.

But she unbent for the ceremony of the pan-drop.

I was summoned to the hearth. Taking a pan-drop from a glass jar, she would place it on the fender and pulverise it with a poker. She turned the fire-iron the wrong way in her hand. Its head was a burnished bronze mushroom. With this she would execute the frivolous indulgence that was the sweet, and I always feared for the precious pieces. It was placed on the whorled corner of that fender and broken like a criminal on the wheel – rendered innocuous for the tender palate of the anxiously waiting youngling.

My only other memory of her concerns her death. When there had been no pan-drop for a day or two I bothered my mother and father to know where Epp had gone to. I can still sense their sad inability to explain in the abstract. So they took me into death's physical presence.

I can vividly recall the total blackness of the room where she was laid out. It was the dead vast and middle of the night – I know precisely how the sentries felt waiting for the apparition of Old King Hamlet's ghost.

We entered the room of death.

Its enveloping silence hung like a tapestry. I stumbled into those heavy invisible folds. The abnormally hushed whispers of my parents still deafen me, years later. A match was struck. There was no electricity in that house of gas-mantles where at that moment there was no shilling to feed the meter. A flaring yellow nova burst the great silent universe of the pit-mirk in which I cringed. Criss-cross patterning of the trestle on which lay a big dark shape. Arms lifting me up. Darkness again, and another match struck. Then the dark inscrutable workmanship of shining oak, the brass mirror of the polished name-plate – Elspeth Marr, her name, her years. That's where she is – in there.

The rest was silence.

Thus early, death made a tangible entry into my universe. Later I would watch a funeral cortege from afar with a wary eye. The hearses and cars wound their way up the green mound of the seaside kirkyard like a procession of shining black beetles that gleamed beneath the sun. When there was to be a funeral, an old town-crier strode solemnly through the streets like a medieval leper, ringing a deep-throated bell. Its iron tongue accompanied his own, that told you the day and the time and the place.

Always a funeral service was held in the house of the departed, where the corpse was duly laid out, ritually subjected to that last longing lingering look – a black procession of eyes, looking down on the lids that veiled eternity – and finally kisted and screwed down. A house of death was always recognisable by its drawn blinds. I often wondered what it would be like to be on the inside of such a fearful house. My time came soon enough. There were several old ones in our family that went the way of all the earth before I had walked upon it for many years. And always my grand-mother would say the same thing: 'And to think we've all to come to it!' It was as if she had just remembered that cloud over the sun that puts all earth's folk in the shadow.

Although my grandmother was a sore sufferer from asthma, my memories of her house are essentially happy ones, memories that I recreate in the story *Aere Perennius*. Her wheezing gray frailty was offset by the simple satisfaction of the homely fare she provided – kail and boiled beef and mashed potatoes; mugs of tea and jeely pieces; and fish in great numbers, herrings and haddocks and cod, and shoals of flatfish to be picked to the bone. She showed me St Peter's thumb-mark on the haddock. She taught me how to gut and fillet. And now, alas, in this age of frozen food in plastic packets, my fish-fingers have become indeed all thumbs!

My grandfather, although he died in his fifties, did not seem old and worn before his time, like his spouse. I remember him instead for his Spanish blue-black hair and deep brown eyes, his gypsy skin. He rolled cigarettes and drank screwtops. He smelled of salt and woodbine. Othello-like, he told me of his travels' history, and I found it passing strange. He sailed the seven seas seventy-seven times, and always he came back with tobacco in his turn-ups.

Between them they gave birth to a generation of shrill, red-lipped aunts, who sang and kissed too hard, and slick-haired uncles, who were always off to catch the bus to the Regal and the Empire picture-houses in Anstruther, with suits double-breasted and acre-wide ties larded with flowers and snakes – such was the fashion – or even, if my grandmother hadn't caught them first at the door, curvaceous ladies, as naked as my innocence.

The pictures and the dancing apart, most of their entertainment was self-made and carried out in the home, in those blessed days before television when families sat down and sang and talked as one. The stories were mostly of sea and sail, and I heard them along with the hearty uncles and the flighty aunts, and the sad-moustached great-uncles and the ancient frail great-aunts. Bent and drooping they were, like flowers heavy with age, their withered heads lolling on the slender stalks of their dry faded bodies.

I remember these stories of yesteryear as easily as I forget the best-sellers of today. The story of tinker Johnny, whom the men of St Monans buried alive for fear of typhoid. He knocked and knocked from inside his coffin (they had taken him for dead at first) but they put him to his grave all the same, and let the earth that they heaped around him soak up his cries. I have included this in the reminiscences of the old grave-digger in a story entitled *Selbie*. Then there was the tale of the One-Gallas Gang, who cut off dogs' heads for fun. But I doubt whether I should wish to give their terrible deeds even a whisper of immortality. Some of my grand-father's own phobias were passed on to me – verbally, if not genet-ically. I could not come to eat whelks after hearing him tell of a seaman's body dragged up in the nets. 'Covered in them it was', he said, 'like shiny black beads sewn into the skin.'

And the crabs that dined on sailors – still they come scrabbling out of the boiling pot to infest my dreams. All bubbling and bulging, and red with rage and terror.

But before long I was out of the day-long protection of kith and kin, and into the wide world of our little village – St Monans of the seagulls.

It was a fishing and boat-building village above all. In those days the boat sheds rang with the sound of the adze and the curing sheds were ecstatic with the reek of newly done kippers. A forest of moving masts jostled in the harbour, a Birnam Wood of propitious omen, and the fish gleamed from pier to pier like stacks of silver bullion. It was the very tail-end of the great herring boom, though nothing compared to what my grandfather must have seen as a boy. I soon came to know a good catch – ninety cran, a hundred cran – and the boats that were likely to make them. Today their names ring round the walls of my brain like names out of scripture – *The True Vine*, *Magdalene*, *The Shepherd Lad*.

The glory has departed. I go back today, smell tar and tangle, try to catch the ghosts of the fishing industry that linger in the smartly coloured lobster-creels and flutter vainly in the meshes of the new nylon nets. The Common Market is alive and well – the old fishing ways, and the men who followed them, are pale shadows of the past.

But the faces remain, the douce Dutch faces of my ancestors; the Nordic seas that glimmer in a pair of Viking eyes; the suns of Spain that burnish that complexion. The ancestral winds of many voyages have written wrinkles into the faces of the fishermen of today. It was ever thus. History gets worked at last into the flesh, like the lines of passage, entered on the log-books of their parchment skins.

Faces. I remember sailors who are now to coral turned, farmers that are kirkyard clay. I remember old wives who kept the secrets of the town about their scrubbed doorsteps – toothless sybils who sat in the sun to stay alive an hour longer, and weave village gossip on the cracked old looms of their tongues. They make their appearance in *The Furies*.

And still in dreams I re-encounter some of them, in the cobbled closes and on the bouldered beaches, where their faces and forms first broke in upon my childhood.

There was the awful man who drowned unwanted kittens. He just dropped them in a pail of water, sat on it, and laughed. He met me in a wynd once, and with a leer informed me that he would cut my head off. I saw no reason to doubt him and fled screaming for my mother. There was the old, cold, gold-earringed sailor who drew me conspiratorially into the folds of his sea-waistcoat, pointed his white buccaneering beard at me, and whispered unto me the strangest sentence I have ever heard: 'I've seen monsoons and typhoons and baboons – and teaspoons!'

These were the eccentrics, whom progress has mostly swept

away. One of them would place his hands on his navy-blue lapels, draw himself up to his full height, and announce with a staggering show of pride, 'I stood where thousands fell!' Later I was told the true meaning of this. In the old days the only public convenience, other than the rocks, was a contraption that jutted out over the back of the harbour wall. A hole in the overhang permitted human excreta to be deposited directly into the sea, as into the moat of a medieval castle. When the tide was out, a few old fishermen might potter about on the rocks beneath, looking for crab bait. This was the inglorious battlefield on which my friend had stood unscathed. And thus the age of affluence has purged away the age of effluence. The old ordure changeth.

And country lore? I once had a very bad boil on my leg that made the limb swell up to twice its size. As I limped along the braes an old man hailed me, and refused to let me go until he had found a snail, which he rubbed on the sore for nearly an hour. Next morning the leg had gone down like a balloon. The fate of the snail is unknown.

The place was ridden with superstitions, of course, and I have woven some of these into *Wine is a Mocker*. There seems little need to say anything of them here. They die hard, like the religions of a place. I use the plural because the St Monans I knew was a polyglot of sects. It was known in the East Neuk as 'The Holy City', its churches as many as the many-tided sea. There were Roman Catholics and Presbyterians and Congregationalists; there were the Pilgrims, who brought God under one another's roofs; there were Open Brethren, Close Brethren, Fergusson's Brethren and Duff's Brethren – indeed any brethren at all that cared to construct a whole theological alphabet out of one undotted iota. There were Baptists and Evangelists, and Jehovah's Witnesses round the doors – never a Mormon in those days. They hell-fired at you in the streets and summoned you to judgement through your letter-box. They spilled out onto the piers where the setting suns turned the tranquil harbour into a lake of fire. This was if you did not come to church.

And if you did come to church, they leaned over their pulpits and pleaded with you to come forward and be saved, until their faces turned purple, and the veins burst out on their brows, under the storm-tossed wrath of their raging white hair. At Sunday School I was asked by a travelling evangelist if I was saved. I might have been about seven at the time. I think I was 'converted' when I was ten.

That was not a true conversion, and so I can never truly be

apostate. The truth is that I *am* a religious person, in the sense that I do not believe that the person now writing these words consists purely of brain and bones and muscles and blood. I cannot believe in the myth of mortality, and it is the blind faith of the atheist which astonishes me, rather than that of the Christian. The strains on my own Christianity are very real. Still, the pull of the old is strong, and the strains of the rock of ages still abide with me, drifting in from the sea of faith (no longer at the full) over the harbour walls of memory, into the haven of the years. Something of the religious complexities of my home can be found in *Not Without Honour*.

Oddly enough I can remember more about my Sunday School than I can recall from all my years in Primary. I went in at one end of that dreary tunnel and came out into the light totally unchanged, except that I had learned the three R's and knew the names of a few capitals and kings. In the coarse curriculum that we followed there was little attempt to educate the imagination. It was administered unto us by bunned and bespectacled old dears who belted us round the bare legs if we did our sums wrong. They were always 'Miss'. I wonder now if any of them had ever known love.

From an image of children wheeling and diving like a playground of gannets and gulls – still in the late forties playing at Messerschmidts and Spitfires – I passed to secondary school in Anstruther, Waid Academy, which I recall with feelings of the deepest gratitude. Most of my teachers were enlightened and humane Scots, who got to the heart of me with insight and sympathy. Mathematics and science I could never understand. Language and literature, history, music and art – these were what I loved. When I discovered a compendium Shakespeare I began reading at page one and read right through to the end. Then I did the same again, five times during my fourth year at school. Thirty-seven plays and a thousand pages five times over in one great intoxicating guzzle. I even swallowed the glossary whole, and I have been drunk on the wine of words ever since. Sweetest Shakespeare, 'tis thou hast ravished me!

Our school chaplain embodied a vanished part of Scotland, and his ghost lingers with sharp sweetness in my senses. A lad o' pairts from Fochabers, Dr George Ogg shawed neeps in the fields, to earn himself the money to keep himself at university, which he finally left with five degrees – M.A., B.Sc., M.Litt., B.D., D.D. An intellectual colossus of a man, he grew old in humble service in Anstruther, where he used to wander around obscurely, just looking, it always seemed to me, for someone to speak to on his own level – which was very difficult. When he died I saw some of his books brought from the sixteenth century manse of the famous James Melville, which he had inhabited. Exercise jotters crammed with Greek-larded sermons and thoughts on evolution had strange mathematical doodles in the margins: the good doctor knew about relativity, perhaps even more, I suspect, than he let on. I picture him now in his long black coat and broad-brimmed black hat, walking against the sands like some incredibly learned cormorant. His bones now mingle, strangely, with those of a princess of Tahiti, who married an Anstruther minister in the last century – the closest Dr Ogg ever came to the uncelibate state. I frequently go back to his grave, and read that string of letters on his headstone. And ponder.

I have not yet written a story with Dr Ogg in it. Perhaps I should wait until I am worthy of it. But then the story would never be written.

Sex takes place against all backgrounds. But I found in my case that the background was not only as important as my sexual awakening, but an integral part of it. I took my girls to woods and streams, gingerly admiring their persons by the shores of the Dylan Thomas-sounding sea. Poetry was the third ingredient in that magical mixture of the abstract and the concrete, the physical and the spiritual, that makes the time of our adolescence into golden days.

I composed my first poems to a girl whose back garden met mine lip to lip, cabbages and curly kail romantically kissing and intertwining, and complete with Pyramus and Thisbe fence. In my wooing of her I enlisted the help of my pet kitten, which she liked to fondle. Sonnets to her were composed with sighs and tucked into the cat's collar, next to the grey fur. Then the pandar pussy would be pushed, purring, through the fence, her bell tinkling the arrival of yet another woeful ballad made to her part-time mistress's untouchable eyebrow. How I envied that cat! Always it came back sonnetless, having enjoyed her favours. But she never replied, or petted *me*. I sincerely hope that she destroyed that awful verse, or better still, that it was somehow eaten by the cat. When her fisherman father was pulled into the boat's winch one day and ground to death, my love was swallowed up in horror. I don't recall seeing her again after that. No doubt I did, but shut her out of my ken, along with the tragedy that hung round her from then on.

When I left school I left Fife too, for I studied at Aberdeen

University and have ever since taught English in Edinburgh schools, principally at George Watson's College, where I have taught since 1972.

For twenty years I have been wishing I could return to Fife, and out of the city, which I so detest. That is probably the main reason why I began writing – as a vehicle to get me out of the town, and into the ideal world of fields and woods, and village and church by the ever-cleansing sea. I am constantly emigrating, through words, to a better place – a kind of verbo-astral travel. At any rate, I decided at the start of the eighties to compose the poems and stories I had been carrying about with me for years, humphing them about as an ever-burgeoning part of my psychological luggage. The stories that follow represent the unpacking of the first suitcase. Some of them, like *Farewell and Adieu* are based on historical events. Others, such as *Earth's Highest Station* or *The Woman and the Waves* are inspired by real people. In the case of stories like *Lilies That Fester*, *Metamorphosis* or *Exorcism*, my imagination may have quickened the dust beneath the stones of the old East Neuk grave-yards, where many a story lies concealed.

I expect that in the eyes of some people much of what I write would be classed as kailyardish and in search of childhood and identity seeking, and it has become very fashionable to decry these nowadays. From the bandwagon of the old régime critics have jumped to that of the avant-garde (though even that has become an entrenched position) praising works of literature to the degree that they succeed in hiding their Scottishness and avoiding sentimental-ity. How sickeningly absurd! For my part, it would be foolish for me to try and write about what I neither know of nor even care for. Hence my frequent returns to the East Neuk, on the wings of the word.

When I return there in the flesh, all too infrequently, I notice the arrival of the modern world in places like St Monans with more than a tinge of reasonable regret. The village, like many such, has been quaintly taken over in part by functionless foreigners. You can return to the village of your youth to discover that the old place no longer has a butcher, or a chemist, or a barber, but that their seaside homes have been nicely done up by the National Trust, to be inhabited briefly by effete antique dealers and fifth-rate film stars. That there are worse encroachments though, can be seen in the title story, *Peace Comes Dropping Slow*.

I regret too the death of language and landscape.

The first is inevitable. Just as the forest leaves fail and fall, so words have their day, wither, and are heard no more. So much so that I have made little attempt to introduce the voices of Fife's rich dialect into these stories. They would not be understood. Even the young Fifers of today call a gull a gull, and not a 'clow', or a 'coorie', or a 'cuttie', or a 'maw'. Nor can they tell you which rock is called Jarsteen, or which reef is Craw Skellie. On the other hand they know all about punk rock and the six million dollar man and all the other fantasies and lies that the television both fabricates and purveys.

The old community has been broken up. The faces in the firelight have faded into the garish new dawn of what is sometimes called progress. The folk culture is dying. The fishing is going the way of the herring it spoliated. The boat-yards are strangely silent. Above all, the religion brought to the East Neuk by St Monan nearly twelve centuries ago is a frailer thing by far than the power that once drove saints to take to the sea, and, like angelicised Vikings, to sail their ship to bless rather than to plunder the benighted peoples of Fife.

Time is taking apart the mosaic, piece by piece. It is my sincere hope that these stories may put back, even for an hour or two, something of the picture.

CHRISTOPHER RUSH

Edinburgh

Peace Comes Dropping Slow

I ARRIVED at Wormiston in the summer of 1975 after twenty gray years of city life.

It was like taking the wings of the morning.

I had left Fife in my teens to go to university, which I attended as if it had been the church. I underwent the capping ceremony as a monk accepts the tonsure. Entering my first school was like crossing the studious cloister's pale; and in the dim religious light of my classroom I began the work of passing out to starved minds the daily bread of Shakespeare, Tennyson, Keats. These miraculous loaves had fed more than fifty times five thousand. Soon the crumbs were dropping thick and fast from my table.

The trouble was that few bothered to pick them up.

'O taste and see!' I said.

Before long I was muttering darkly about artificial pearls and perfectly genuine swine. How had the brightness fallen from the air?

I suppose that youngsters whose hands are destined one day to be filling in your tax forms and your teeth, will find little use for poetry. Most of the pupils I tried to shape were already cast in that dead mould. I suppose too that growing older among generations of youngsters that bloom perennially whilst you wither has the effect of isolating you, like a tired Tiresias. How long until the wood of the desks enters your soul? Until the chalk starts flowing in your bloodstream?

But what had seeped into me most of all, I think, was the world, and it was a poison my system resisted. My days were perfumed by the most exquisite arrangements of words and deeds. At nights I came home and tried to connect them with the rottenness borne out by newspapers and the television. Starvation and disease, pollution and politics loomed ever larger than literature in my midnight meditations, and slowly disillusionment darkened my sky. The world was a disaster, books a barren irrelevance. Poetry was a web of beautiful lies. I made up my mind to return to the innocence and truth of land and sea. From now on my lake-isle of Innisfree would not be made of words: I would find one and live in it. Living out a truth would not be escaping from it, I decided, and I pictured my nine bean-rows and my hive for the honey bee, beautiful in the bee-loud glade.

That is how I came to give up my teaching post. I rented the farm cottage on the promontory at Fifeness, where the land thrust its prow into the waves like a Viking longship, hungry for the new.

Other than the farmer I was the only human soul for two miles around. I had sea and solitude and the bright ring of the seasons shining outside my window. The work on the farm kept me conscious of that cycle, which I had almost forgotten about in town.

Not that I had anything to do with the farm outside my tenancy – to begin with, that is. I lived by gathering whelks, and taking them up to St Andrews for carriage to London and abroad. In my old life I wouldn't have thought it possible to keep a cat on what I earned from the whelks. But the compensations, let me tell you, were well worth it.

My day began with its highlight – breakfast. What is for most folk a somewhat dim affair turned out to be the glory of my new life. Summer was gold-plating the sea that year, and while the morning radio sent Mozart dancing over the firth – (I allowed myself music) – I sat by the open window smoking my pipe and waiting for Ecksy to arrive with my breakfast.

Ecksy was the milkman.

But his milk rounds were just the limbs and outward flourishes of his trade. All his life he had worked the small dairy farm up at Ribbonfield. Apart from his cows and his hens up there, three withered old aunts, two deaf and one dumb, were all he had for company. And company was what Ecksy sought most in the world, like water in the desert. So when he brought in the milk he always brought himself as well, and a gathering of gossip from the day before. Sometimes he stayed for an hour or more.

Ecksy rose at four o'clock to milk his own cows. He produced just enough to provide for the parish of Crail and a sprinkling of cottages, like mine. Even so, there were a good many folk who never tasted their morning milk until four in the afternoon.

It all depended on whether you lived on the north or the south side of the Golf Tavern. If you lived on the north side, as I did, your milk came early. But when Ecksy's cart arrived at the Golf, his horse would have stopped under any conditions, whether Ecksy had felt wet or dry. Between opening and closing times he abandoned his calling for the stronger call of beer, while those on the south side made do with yesterday's milk, and stormed in their teacups.

Sometimes– not very often – Ecksy overdid it, and the south side milk was never delivered. Then the three aunts would come clucking and croaking down from Ribbonfield to take the cart home, with Ecksy lying in the back in a disordered bed of bottles, snoring loudly.

Eventually most of the wrong-siders got round to strolling up to the idle cart and helping themselves to their own milk. The coppers rattled into the old tin box that the bairns tried to plunder at piece-time. Meanwhile he fleeted the time carelessly in his world of amber, spanned by the rainbow pleasure. At the end of it, he sat with a tumbler of whisky, which was his pot of gold.

Anyway I was one of the lucky ones. In fact I was Ecksy's first call. I like rising early, and that first summer it was a joy to be up and ready for his coming, while the sun's golden pitcher was breaking over the sea, and the barley was bright with dew.

I said that breakfast was the highlight of my day.

It was Ecksy who was the making of it. His tongue chattered like Tennyson's stream, always adding new sparkle to life's fleeting debris, polishing the pebbled bed of memory.

But it was the milk and eggs he brought – these were gifts from the gods. Had I been a south-sider I'd have waited till the crack of doom for those eggs, that milk. I have never seen the like of them. The milk came in a good old-fashioned bottle, not one of these cardboard containers that sends the milk in six different directions over the table. Every bottle of it looked as though a tub of thick double-cream had been wedged inside the neck – the layer went halfway down the bottle. I used to scoop out that precious seam into a separate container. Even the ordinary milk at the bottom tasted like nectar, and porridge and corn flakes were transformed beneath it. An apotheosis for the sum of ten pence.

Then there were the eggs. They were like great brown bombs, but with innocent freckled faces. In the frying pan they burst harmlessly in an ecstasy of goodness, and their great golden suns would be-dazzle the stove, the whites rippling round their yellow orbs like huge coronas. Just one of these eggs was a meal fit for a king.

'A fine mornin'!' Ecksy would shout, as he came clattering into the cottage like a burn in spate. He put down the eggs and milk on the kitchen table and poured himself a cup of tea. And for the next hour his red face would be crinkling into shapes of glee and horror as he rattled off the news of the little world.

One morning he brought honey, still in the comb.

'I didn't know you kept bees as well, Ecksy', I said, my mouth turning to water at the sight and touch of the golden ambrosia.

'Oh aye', he said. 'Had bees up at the farm for years. I've always been meaning to give them up, but I've got kind of attached to them now, ever since the naked lady.'

'What's that?' I said.

The faded blue eyes rolled boldly in his head, and for a twinkling he was a bright old buccaneer.

'Well, it was like this, you see.

I was inside the milk-shed this afternoon – some years back. Washing out bottles, I was. Suddenly I hears screams. I runs out, and here's this fine bit fluff going fair frantic by one o' the hives, and the bees round her like she was jam. She must've come in for eggs and got interested in the honey.

By the time I got to her the wee deils were inside her clothes and God knows where else. She was wearing one of these loose summer frocks, you see.

Well, I just gripped her and ripped every stitch off her back in one go. Then right into the cattle trough with her. That got rid o' the bees.

I picked her up then and carried her dripping wet into the house. You should've seen the old wives' faces. That was the sweetest honey those bees ever gave me! The old ones took charge o' her after that though, which was just as well, I'm telling you. That was worth a sting or two and no mistake.'

After which Ecksy would move on to the affairs of the wider world, who was in and who was out, learnedly dissecting the butterflies of fashion and delving into the riddle of existence as if he were one of God's spies. People like Ecksy, I thought, would wear out daily the packs and sects of great ones that ebb and flow by the moon.

The shape of my day was settled by the tides, my only masters. I obeyed them as unquestioningly as they followed the pull of the moon. If the tide happened to be in during the morning, I might walk the mile into Crail or cycle up to St Andrews for some shopping. Or I'd ramble up to the woods at Redwells, or write up the nature diary I'd begun.

When the tides were out I would go down to the rocks with my sack and bucket and do my day's gathering. Because I was following a natural cycle and not a clock, I felt blessedly free from the curse of routine, that heavy weight of hours that chains people down.

It was a ten minute walk from the cottage to the shore – the length of three fields. They were bordered by a ditch that ran all the way down to the sea, and was wild with flowers that summer – poppies and daisies, campion, cornflowers and blue vetch. How I loved that floral hem! Every morning I accorded it the admiration that Herrick lavished upon Julia's clothes. And every morning seemed to bring forth a greater glory. Green corn and golden barley hung hushed and still in the hot haze of early August, with its close, creamy skies. Lines of daisies swept the fields like silent breakers, and the red mouths of poppies breathed their heavy perfumes into the air as I passed along. In the distance lay the sea, its blue skirts swished far back to uncover spoils for the early morning seeker.

As I broke the skyline the sea birds would rise in complaint, like a white snow-cloud bursting, then settle together again. Eventually they became used to my solitary appearances. Down among the rocks I received the sea breeze like a benediction as I bowed my head to my chosen task.

At that time of year the whelks lay out on the rocks like polished black jewels, scattered from the sea's inexhaustible treasure chest. Sometimes the side of a skellie would be encrusted with them, and I swept them into my bucket like a diamond thief raking loot from a vault. Murmuring miles of sea surrounded me as I worked, and close at hand smaller whisperings came from rock pools and the glistening seaweeds. I drank in solitude like a wine I had craved for all my life and never known. Conversation would have been an irrelevance here. The sea rendered all talk trivial and absurd.

Naturally things weren't always so idyllic.

Summer faded like a dream into dawn, and the ears of barley began to listen, and whisper restlessly on their stalks. Combine harvesters squatted on the horizon like great red beetles, come to devour the beauty of the earth. Soon I was striding down the road between ravaged fields. Daisies lay strewn across the spears of stubble like deflowered virgins, bedaubed with poppy blood.

It was then that I heard a crisper, more metallic sound in the breaking waves, that heralded the arrival of frost. The crabs on the shoreline became sluggish and careless, I noticed, and the whelks crawled closer beneath the boulders, sought the sanctuary of the seaweeds. I had to lift and tear apart the dark, dripping veils, and take my innocent prey by force.

The sea's face turned gray. And as the geese ebbed off south and the shelducks left the coast, the raven wing of winter swept the world.

When that happened the whelks disappeared altogether from sight, into the deepest, darkest chambers of rock pools. I bared my arms then, in the icy mornings, and for long minutes at a time I had to wear an invisible gauntlet of clear cold water. My arms freezing and on fire to the elbows, I fumbled with the bolts and shackles of boulders and brine, behind which my livelihood now locked itself in meagre twos and threes.

But this was also the season of fireside delights.

In the long nights I would sit at the hearth among steaming clothes and driftwood, listening to woodland murmurs rising from the voices of the logs as they rustled and sang. Their twittering little tongues were my fireside companions. In their changing colours I saw black winters give way to golden summers, and these in turn to the blood-red leaves and sunsets of autumn. For relaxation I smoked my pipe, drank a little whisky, and listened to my favourite composers on the radio and the cassette recorder. Tchaikovsky and Rachmaninov – I liked them in winter particularly; they took me through the great Russian steppes. And Tallis and Byrd – their masses lifted me out of this world altogether, out of the sphere of things visible and familiar.

Long after I had gone to bed that winter, I lay propped up on my pillows, the curtains wide apart, watching the silent constellations pass my window, an army beautiful with banners that glittered until dawn.

When I came out of that black burnished tunnel of winter and into the light of spring, I felt as fresh and regenerate as the snowdrop. The whelks began to creep out of their hiding places again and offer themselves to my chill white fingers. Battalions of green spears thronged through the earth, thrusting back the darkness. The stars of the new season fluttered over the sea.

Already I had dismissed the calendar. I knew that spring was coming from the contained quietness in the atmosphere, a stillness that I knew to be different from September or November. With the winds falling away at sunset I noticed sounds coming from a very long way off. The evening call of the partridge was unmistakable, and blackbirds, thrushes and larks began to be heard. By the middle of February the shelducks had returned.

In fact it was the change in my own attitude to February which astonished me most. In schools, and no doubt in a thousand other places, February is usually thought of as the dreich and gloomy month, when absolutely nothing happens. Down on the shore, in the humblest rock pool, everything seemed to be happening. The water, no longer muddy with gales, became crystal clear, so that I could see the tiniest blobs of life suddenly respond to the change in light and temperature. A great movement was afoot there. The waves burst pale green and white – I had never seen that greenness at any other time. And as the bracing winds of March died out, leaving the ragged clouds in peace once more, the great pageant of the migrant birds passed by – swallows and swifts flitting out of nowhere, ducks and diving birds bobbing on the water, gannets ploughing up the firth. April unfolded like a tapestry.

Last of all, the woodlands listened to the call of spring, and answered in a flurry of green voices. The nights began to lengthen. When I took a late-night walk down to the shore, I noticed the first faint afterglow of sun still visible on the horizon. I felt, towards the end of my first year at Wormiston, as if I had purged myself of all the extraneous filth that had clogged up my spiritual system for twenty years.

Summer swung round sweetly to my will.

That was my idyll.

I have described it as intensely and carefully as I can, for I am afraid I am no longer living it. I can vividly recall the moment things started to go wrong.

It was a breathless summer's night. I had been listening to a talk on the radio. When my programme finished I opened the windows, put the lights out, and slipped into bed with a bottle of claret at my side – a birthday present from a friend.

I was leaning over to switch off the radio when a velvety BBC voice informed me that there was to be a broadcast of Byrd's Five Part Mass, to end at midnight. This Tudor church piece was one of my supreme favourites. Quickly I uncorked the bottle and poured myself a glass of the claret. Then I turned the volume down to the merest whisper and lay back.

Soon the serenity of a bygone age was washing over me like the hush of a distant sea; a tide of faith sweeping in from centuries ago, bearing me off to the foam of the stars that spattered the depths of space. I sipped my wine slowly, holding lost summers in my mouth in moments of timeless fragrance. The waves of holy words drowned out my questionings. Kyrie eleison. Christe eleison. Kyrie eleison.

Seconds later I was sitting upright in bed, stiff as a post, my ears bombarded by a high-pitched bleeping sound that seemed to be coming from the direction of the sea. It only lasted several seconds, but it had fairly destroyed the atmosphere created by the music. I lay back disgruntled, and concentrated again on Byrd. But in less than a minute the bleep came back again, loud and clear. For all I knew it could have been going on all night, and now, with the windows open and the radio turned down, it had only just attracted my attention. Or perhaps a passing ship was engaged in some kind of manoeuvre. One thing was certain, I couldn't banish the sound from my brain. The pattern that unfolded was too cleverly timed for that – neither long enough nor short enough between the bleeps, and every bleep lasting nearly five seconds.

I turned the volume higher and tried to give myself over to the music. It was no good. When the thing, whatever it was, was not bleeping, I found myself waiting for it, and counting the bars of rest – forty-five seconds of expectant silence, then five seconds of that hysterical humming inside the walls of my skull.

The music struggled into its final section.

Agnus dei, qui tollis peccata mundi, miserere nobis. Dona nobis pacem.

I had been robbed of that disembodied serenity which is the gift of sixteenth century religious music to the ravished listener. I rose and shut the windows. I would have to do without fresh air if this affair was going to last any length of time.

But even that did not beat the bleeping. Its strident regularity was now subdued, but unignorable. I had become used at Wormiston to the soothing balm of silence. Now even that small pin-point of sound, piercing the night, probed me as if I were an open wound.

I rose and stepped outside in my pyjamas.

The milky way hung over the cottage like a huge bough, apple-blossomed with stars. Not a breath of wind stirred them. The cornfields were asleep. In the distance I could hear the hush of the sea, with now and then a wave, dipping into time.

Then came the sound again, this time as bright and blatant as a magnesium flare, now that I was in the open. I walked round to the gable end of the house and looked out to sea, trying to locate the source of my sore distraction. The two firths of Forth and Tay melted in a flow of silver, beneath the afterglow. The sea was a dark mirror into which you could peer forever, a silent witness to eternity. Alternately, the lights from the May Island and the Bell Rock flashed my shadow swiftly against the gable-end of the whitewashed cottage.

It was only after several minutes that I understood what was missing. There was no North Carr lightship.

Throughout my lifetime the little red lightship had bobbed its warning a mile off the point at Fifeness. A crimson cork by day, a cluster of bright stars by night, it had kept many a seaman out of the slavering teeth of the deadly Carr reef. Now it was simply not there.

What would a London dweller feel if he woke up one morning to find that Nelson's column, or the Houses of Parliament had just disappeared? Well, that was how I felt. I just stood there, staring.

Then I saw that there was a tiny little light, to the south-east of where the North Carr had been. I brought out my binoculars and fastened on the alien star that had swum into my ken overnight. The light was attached to some kind of buoy, it seemed. And that was undoubtedly the place that my unlovely siren was wailing from. I went back to bed and managed to drift off, sleepily hoping that if the North Carr was in for servicing, it wouldn't be gone for too long. Noisy nights were not a welcome substitute.

But when Ecksy appeared in the morning he brought in bad tidings with the milk and eggs.

'The North Carr's away', he announced.

'I know that well enough', I said.

'Do you not like your new replacement then?'

'I'll be glad when the boat's back', I said. 'Just listen to that din. How long do you think the ship'll be away?'

'Away?'

Ecksy's face crinkled.

'Are you not listening to what I'm telling you? It's replaced. Gone for good. It's tied up now in Anster harbour, and it's to bide there as a museum. That thing out there is here for keeps.'

I stared at him. So this pestiferous little insect buzzing out in the bay was to sting me to distraction forever. I couldn't believe it.

'Ecksy', I said, 'I want you to post a letter for me.'

While Ecksy drank his tea I wrote off to the Northern Lighthouse Board expressing my outrage. I said that I was not writing as a fanatical environmentalist against the pollution of peace – simply as an ordinary member of the public who wanted to live and work and eat and sleep in silence.

I got back a courteous enough letter, telling me how expensive it was in these inflationary times to maintain even a small crew on a tiny lightship, and how much cheaper it was to use this bleeping buoy. The warning signal was set to sound continuously, fair weather or foul, quite literally every minute of the day, every day of the year. And the beauty of it was that it needed no attention.

So that was the price of safety in time of recession. For me it was the unkindest cut of all. Naturally I grew used to the signal after a time, but on calm windless nights it came through me like a needle. I listened to music as if through toothache. I took fewer walks down to the shore.

The infuriating thing about it was that in wild weather I could hardly hear the thing at all. But at the quietest times it bleeped its poison shrilly into my ears. The sunniest morning and balmiest evening were ripped apart. The best night automatically became the worst. Gradually the gold of silence rusted until I could not remember how bright it had been. But for the Northern Lighthouse Board it was just another noise that the world would have to assimilate – and forget.

That winter I wore my disappointment like an old wound that troubled me on certain days but at other times was just a part of living. Eventually I accepted things as they were – the shores of my silence were polluted, but there were other things that were unspoiled.

Then one morning Ecksy brought in the paper with more bad news. Old Simpson, the pig farmer across the way, had applied to the Fife council for permission to convert his land into a caravan site for one thousand caravans. I looked at the notice blackly and thought of the future. First the silence, now the solitude. How long would it be before they took away the sea?

'What's the trouble?' I asked. 'His family have run that place for generations.'

'Money', said Ecksy. 'He's losing it fast, so he says.'

'You mean he can't get it fast enough', I said.

'There's more to it than that', said Ecksy. 'There's foreign pigs coming in at cheaper prices. Simpson can't stand the competition.'

'There's local pigs too', I said. 'Simpson must know how this would ruin Fifeness. This place is practically a bird sanctuary.'

'Aye, but you canna bury your head in the sand altogether. You've got to move with the times.'

There was a short silence.

'I've had a bit of an offer myself', Ecksy added.

'What kind of offer?'

He screwed up his face.

'Well, it's a bit complicated and I'll have to sleep on it. I'll tell you when I know more about it.'

There was a longer silence.

'Anyway', Ecksy said, 'the council might turn down Simpson's request.'

On the Monday morning following, Ecksy didn't appear at breakfast time. The tide was just right for gathering, so I left him a note and went down to the shore.

There was a strange smell in the air, I thought, as I tramped along the road, feeling a distinct lack of one of Ecksy's eggs glowing in my wintry stomach. Something else about the quality of the morning made me feel vaguely uneasy. I couldn't tell what at the time.

When I crossed the shoulder of the hill, overlooking the shore, my insides twisted themselves into an icy knot. I could see at once what had caused that smell.

It was oil.

The shoreline was black with it. Somewhere out in the North Sea perhaps there had been a spillage, and the slick had caught the tip of Fife as it glided southwards. There had been a high tide; the thick black treacle had spread its clutches right up to the foreshore.

Dropping my bucket I ran along the ridge to Randerston cliffs, from where I could see all the beaches along to St Andrews. I saw them all right – like black mourning ribbons unfurled the length of the coast. Come unto these yellow sands, some perverted Caliban of the sea had whispered to that black sea-serpent. And inwards it had slithered, covering the golden beaches with the black gold of the times that glistened wickedly beneath the pale morning sun.

I walked slowly down to the rocks.

It was a savage scene. Scores of sea birds fluttered feebly in their sticky pall. Others sat there dumbly, like silhouettes, awaiting a certain death. It was then that I realised what it had been about the morning that had bothered me earlier – its birdless silence. Not a gull cried. Silence lay on the morning like a shroud, deathly, invisible. Even the sea-bells had stopped swinging, the water no longer flowed. Only the bleeper sounded its alien knell across the firth, breaking in on the horror.

As for my livelihood, I saw it lying dead and buried under that disgusting mess. There was no point even trying to calculate how long it would take to clean up. It would take months initially, but the effects would still be around years later. I turned my back on it and trudged up the road, vaguely working out in my head how long I could survive on my savings.

When I neared the cottage I saw a lorry disappearing in a cloud of exhaust fumes. Looking down at my doorstep I saw two cartons of milk. I picked one up in my oily fingers. It had 'Kirkcaldy Dairies Ltd' printed on it in bright orange letters. Not even thinking about what it could mean, I ate a miserable breakfast and switched on the radio for news of the disaster.

A tanker on its way to Methil had run into difficulties. No one knew what had caused the leakage, but investigation was under way. The accident had taken place overnight and no warning had been possible.

I changed my clothes and headed for the Golf Tavern.

The Golf was the forenoon haunt of a few retired fishermen, who made it their howff until closing time passed them back to their empty cottages, or to gather in groups at the pier head. Their hard hands had once held fast to the helm, hauled on the nets in the great days of the herring. They had gripped the tiller through all the seas that life had flung at them. Now they lifted pint-pots in their shaky fingers. One or two of them still took out their little yawls from time to time, hugging the harbour for an hour or more, or pottered about among the skellies looking for lobsters and partans. Mostly they rested their ruined bellies against the polished brass of the bar rail. From there they sailed off each morning on a tide of beer, misted over with a few nips of whisky.

It was busier than usual when I walked in, but a lot quieter. The old men's eyes were lost in their tankards. When they talked at all it was only about what had happened. But they spoke about it under their breaths, as if they were discussing a funeral.

Only one old man raised his voice.

'Sheer bloody greed', he kept saying. 'It's the lust for money that has killed this coast. Folk nowadays'll stop at nothing to get it, and it'll end bad, that's for sure.'

I joined them in silence.

Half an hour later Ecksy appeared. But it was on an old bike he parked outside and not his horse and cart. I asked him what was going on.

It was, he told me, all to do with the Common Market.

First he had had a letter. Then two officials, Government men, had visited him at the farm and offered him a good price to sell his milk, which was seemingly too cheap in any case, to one of the big Fife dairy firms. The milk was now being picked up by a van and taken to Kirkcaldy. There it was mixed in with the produce from the bigger dairies, who charged a higher price for their pint. I winced at the thought of that cream of the gods merging into anonymity with the insipid fluid I had poured over my porridge that morning.

'Of course, what they really want is for me to stop producing altogether', Ecksy said.

I asked him why.

'Well', said Ecksy, 'they've offered me £450 for each beast, if I slaughter them, and that's double the price just now. The way I see it, I'm coming up to retiral age anyway. With a herd the size o' mine I'd make a tidy bit o' money on that deal.'

'You can't weigh ready cash against a whole way of life', I said.

'I've told you already', he said, 'a body's got to move wi' the times he's living in.'

'Ah, the times, the times', I said.

We drank in silence for a little.

After a time Ecksy said, 'Did you ken that there were once over forty wee dairy farms like mine in Fife? And now there's just three.'

'Or maybe just two', I said.

'Aye, maybe just the two at that.'

Ecksy did retire, later in the year. And he made himself a lot of money. He had about fifty cows, and with the cash he got for having them slaughtered he came into twenty thousand pounds.

He had never handled so much money in his life, and he couldn't handle it now. Ever since he was a youngster his pattern had been the same, rising in the first light of morning to milk the cows that linked him to the community. His relation with that community was woven into the fabric of his being. He had never been known to take a holiday, not even on New Year's Day. Now he was a man at a loss with himself. He still rose at the same time every morning and sat around the house all day, staring at his crooning old aunts and getting under his own feet.

That's how he came to take to the drink in a really serious way. He had always enjoyed his daily tipple, as I said. But most of the time he had been a canny enough drinker. Now his sprees became harder and longer, and he came back at nights for more, buying drinks for all and sundry and making a pest of himself, until he was finally banned from the Golf altogether.

After that he bought the hard stuff from the licensed grocers and took it home with him to keep under his bed. All day he sat around the deserted sheds, where he used to milk the cows, hiding from his aunts and drinking himself into blackouts. Everybody said he wouldn't see the spring.

He didn't. But as it happened it wasn't the drink which finally carried him off. It was cancer.

It started off one day with a sore leg. He limped around for a fortnight until he couldn't stand the pain any longer. They sent him to the Royal Infirmary in Dundee. He was there for two months but there was nothing to be done. He lay down like blotting paper and let the cancer run through him.

They let him out in January. Ten days later nature accomplished what alcohol would have achieved artificially. Ecksy's golden handshake, offered by the world, was a tiny touch of death.

The winter wore away.

There was nothing to be gathered from that shrouded shore except the carcasses of birds and the dead detritus of sea life. Environmental scientists moved around like moon men, weirdly helmeted and spreading chemicals. I stayed in a lot to begin with, or took walks in the country. Then, when one of his casual workers left, I began to do odd jobs for old Laing, the farmer. I didn't like him much – he was as tight as a drum – but I needed the little money he paid me.

When spring broke through, the black death had begun to disintegrate. The balmy purring of outboard motors soothed the forlorn mornings, as the old lobster-men came out to do their shopping among the seagulls. A few whelks crept cautiously off the shelves of the sea and laid themselves on the shore's rocky counter.

But the ban on whelks wasn't yet lifted. So I did some more menial work for Laing – lifting up stones after the ploughing. It was boring, but out of these stones came bread.

One morning the tractor man took the plough right up to the very edge of the path, ploughing away the border where my wild flowers had grown.

'What did you do that for?' I asked him.

'Mr Laing's instructions', he said.

'But why?'

He stared at me.

'Why do you think? A yard of ground running for half-a-mile – that's a fair bit of money, you know. Anyway, why are you so interested in a ditch?'

I lost more than my floral border that summer, though. The price of whelks went down drastically. The dealer in St Andrews said that there was a glut of Irish whelks on the market. I earned just over half the money for doing the same work I had done a year ago. Another thing was local unemployment. When the schools broke up in July and another wave of jobless youngsters spilled into the towns, the whelk gathering was a stop-gap for a fair number of them. Most of them drew dole money as well as their undeclared earnings from the whelks. They also brought their transistors down among the rocks, and on some mornings Radio One blared from over a dozen different points along the shore.

When autumn set in I offered to help Laing with the tattie gathering. He said I could drive one of the tractors and take the loads up to the farm. I was glad to be given this job because my own work at the whelks was a back-bending occupation, and lately financial forces had kept me at it for longer each day.

It was a crisp morning in October when we started. Looking back from my high seat I watched with satisfaction as the gleaming blades twirled and sank into the wounded earth. The scent of newly dug potatoes rose out of the rich darkness and the gatherers stooped to their task.

The weather kept fine. A fortnight later we were halfway through the second field.

After the first dreel of the third Monday morning my cart was heaped high. I drove the tractor up the road towards the bin. As I neared the farmhouse Laing stepped out of his door. He held up his hand.

'Wait', he said.

I stopped the engine.

'I'll tell you what I want you to do now', he said. 'I want you to take this load down past the bottom field and dump it on the foreshore.'

I looked at him.

'Can I ask you why, Mr Laing?'

The old farmer's face tightened.

'Can I ask you if it's any of your damned business?'

'I'm sorry', I said, 'I'm just interested.'

'Well, you'll be interested to know that the rest of that field that you're on has to be dumped in the same way. So get on with it.'

'I don't believe it', I said.

'Look!' Laing was growing red in the face. 'Don't you meddle in matters that don't concern you.'

'But it does concern me', I said. 'It concerns me a lot.'

'Right', he said. 'For your information this is a matter of economics. The price of potatoes is to be kept up right now, for reasons that have absolutely nothing to do with you. For your further information I'm being paid to dump them, and you're being paid to carry out my orders, so no-one's going to lose out. Now get on with it! You'll be late enough as it is for your next load.'

'Mr Laing', I said, 'Why don't I drive them straight over to old Simpson's, for pig food? His place is actually nearer than the foreshore. Rather than dump them down there, they can do some good at his place.'

'Start driving. And do as you're told!'

'But this is crazy! There's a man over there who can hardly afford to feed his own pigs, so he says. You are in a position to help him at no cost or trouble to yourself.'

'Right, get down off that tractor.'

I made way for him as he stormed past me into the driver's seat.

'I'll do the job myself', he shouted, starting up the engine. 'And as for you, your work on the farm is finished. And you can get your arse out of that cottage!'

'My lease runs till the last day of December', I told him.

'And I won't be renewing it!' he roared. 'Now get to hell!'

The tractor turned and lumbered off towards the sea.

Laing kept his word.

He sent me an official letter informing me that the lease on the cottage would not be renewed into the next year. I stayed until the very end, and saw the last light of 1977 thicken over Wormiston. Then I stayed the night at the house of an old school friend in Anstruther. Next morning I travelled back to my mother's house in town, to start looking for a job. I had left it saying that small was beautiful. I had come back thinking that it only made the ugliness seem worse.

Early in the new year I heard that old Simpson had been denied permission to build a caravan site on his land. I began to think that the world had not quite lost its wits. Then a week later I understood the real reason. There was a leak to the press that Fifeness had been ear-marked by the Government as the site for a new American nuclear missile base. The suggestion was so strenuously denied by the politicians that everyone could see it was true.

The new base was to be built on the land belonging to both Simpson and Laing. They must have been paid a high price, I thought – many pieces of silver.

Lilies that Fester

'I DON'T like it, Mr Erskine, I don't like like the idea one little bit.'

Sandy Munro, the session clerk of Kilrenny Kirk, shook his mass of white curls disapprovingly, and his face furrowed with uneasiness as he faced the minister he had served so loyally for the past twenty-seven years.

They were standing in the kirk's musty little vestry, and the elders were awaiting session in the adjacent room, where the meeting was due to begin. Sandy greatly resented the personal appeal that was now being made to him beneath the ecclesiastical counter. It was deeply unfair of the minister, he felt, thus to request his complaisance in a scheme which in any case he felt to be both nonsensical and unseemly.

The reverend gave an iron smile.

'I understand your feelings, Sandy', he said, 'but all the same I should be very glad if at the meeting you would show some little support for my plan, or at least refrain from any criticisms that might give the lead to a possible move by the session to thwart it.'

Sandy towered in embarrassed silence. He was a monolith of a man, with the gentleness of a violet. His enormous hands hung awkwardly by his sides, trembling slightly, and his face began to redden.

'Minister, I ... I don't ... I can't support you in this, I'm sorry. It's seldom we've not been of one mind, I know, but I just cannot see eye to eye with you on this one. In my humble opinion the thing is hardly proper, and I should have to say so. I'm sorry.'

The minister removed his spectacles, began to polish them, and spoke very quietly.

'Sandy, some time ago I engaged you and your men to carry out a great deal of work for me on the manse.'

'I know very well, Mr Erskine, and don't think I'm not grateful. . . .'

'Then show your gratitude man.' The silky tone curled itself round the other's hesitation.

'It's work that will last you for years to come, as you are well aware. But it's not work that is absolutely vital.'

And he added in a much tighter voice, 'Indeed, for both of us it is something of a luxury, is it not?'

Sandy sighed and relaxed his titan's strength with a beaten and baffled air. The truth was that the manse was no ordinary manse; it was a sixteenth century mansion house, standing in much need of renovation. The minister was no ordinary minister; his ancestors had owned the house and estate for hundreds of years before entering the church, and the tradition of lairds in the cloth had continued in Kilrenny for centuries. Mr Erskine was, to put it plainly, a moneyed minister. And old Sandy was no ordinary builder either – for that was his trade; he was a superb craftsman, with a medieval mason's passion for anonymous labour in the service of stone.

In past years though, he had found little scope for his devotional urge to answer the lapidary calling. Erecting a red-brick public convenience for the local caravan site, or fixing some poor old body's window-cords for nothing – that was the diet to which his sensitive palate had grown accustomed; and he had been on the point of paying off the four men who worked for him when the minister had stepped in and offered him the work on the manse. The monetary rewards brought forth smiles from Sandy's worldly wife, who cared for stones only when turned to bread by the miracle of her husband's art; the aesthetic remuneration was what mattered most to the man.

'Well, Sandy?'

His pastor and benefactor waited with uncompromising grace.

'Well, so long as the others are in approval. . . .'

The minister smiled. He knew that his session clerk's fellow elders would follow their leader. They were the heavenly stars in the hamlet's tiny firmament, but Sandy was their primum mobile, and they were not much moved by intelligences of their own. Moreover, although he had resorted to mild blackmail, Mr Erskine was relieved that his chief elder had not actually voiced that protestation, perhaps because he had been sufficiently human to succumb to it.

The two men passed together into the panelled session room.

'A lily-pond!' spluttered James Gourlay, of the fabric committee.

The meeting had broken up and the minister was in the vestry putting on his hat and coat.

'A lily-pond – in a kirkyaird fu' o' decent Christian folk! An' wi' gowdfish!' he added, as if this last item was one which quite clearly added insult to the injury of any folk whatsoever, Christian or heathen, living or dead.

'I've nivver heard the like', he went on. 'Whit in God's name possessed ye, Sandy, tae let the man awa wi' sic a nonsense?'

The nine men who made up the session were standing in a circle just outside the main door of the church. It was late March and well after seven, and a bitter wind was coming off the sea. Sandy was hatless, his white hair blowing into his eyes. He did not return the stares of his audience as he spoke.

'Ach, it's not such a bad thing as you might imagine, James. We've got to move with the times if we're going to attract younger folk into the kirk these days.'

He paused, sensing the lack of conviction in his own voice was easily detectable.

'Look, I'll not make out that I'm over fond of the scheme myself, but I did think there was some sound logic in what Mr Erskine was saying in there. Now why not give the man at least some credit for trying something new? Do you know what the figure in the rolls is down to now?'

Gourlay looked from the ruffled session clerk to the faces of his friends and followers. They were shivering in the darkening wind, buttoning up their thick overcoats, and in spite of their disquiet, not really wishing to prolong the debate in the open air.

'Ye've gane gyte!' Gourlay persisted, 'the baith o' ye, if ye ask me, plain saft in the heid! An' ye'll rue the day, the twa o' ye, oh aye, you mark my words, nae guid'll come o't, I'm telling ye.'

He raised a gloved forefinger prophetically.

The Reverend Erskine now emerged from the church, smiling. He was well pleased with the success he had achieved in the dumbfounded silence of the session room. At the formal 'any other business' query, he had announced to the stony faces of these pillars of the kirk that it was his intention to give their place of worship a new look for the coming summer, and indeed for all time.

Kilrenny Kirk was well situated, there was no doubt about that. It stood on the west side of a burn that was trimmed with hawthorn bushes. The graveyard itself was a mound which sloped away down to this burn on the one side. On the north side it was skirted by a gentle green sward which the locals called the Commontry. To the east and scarcely two hundred yards away glinted the sea. The whole was surrounded by a dyke, which, on the three sides facing the main coast road and the village streets was so low that an entirely uninterrupted view of the ancient and picturesque church would have been afforded, but for one thing – the session house.

The old session house was a grim, grey obstruction which squatted toad-like, directly in front of the kirk on its west side. It had been erected in 1762 – the date was carved on the lintels of the door – and had served the administrative conclaves of the parish church for nearly a hundred years. In the nineteenth century a session room had been built into the church itself without altering its external structure, and the dismal old out-building had been used for some time as a store room and finally closed up altogether. Not one of the Erskines since had had the initiative to have it demolished, despite the fact that its uncompromisingly malevolent bulk quite spoiled the aspect of the old kirk, from both near and far.

It was the wish of the Erskine now officiating that this ugly obstruction be removed forthwith, and that it be replaced by something altogether more attractive. Instead of that lugubrious monstrosity he proposed that there should be created something which would speak in nature's own tongue of the loveliness of God the maker. What he suggested was a lily-pond – with goldfish, to catch the sunlight and dispel the shadow of evil; to mirror the laughter of Sunday School infants, and to turn the thoughts of the old from the gloom of graves to the loveliness of life.

There was no possibility that these operations would disturb any existing graves, for that portion of the church ground had never been used for burials as far back as the records extended, and in any case the session house had stood there for over two hundred years. So that, unless the session saw any objection to their minister's plan, he moved that it be implemented straight away, the work to be carried out by members of the fabric committee, who were none other than two of Sandy Munro's employees, plus Sandy himself, who doubled as its chairman. The minister magnanimously reckoned that these two could easily be spared from the work on the manse during the two or three months that the entire job would probably take to complete.

Mr Erskine had then turned to the session clerk, who always sat next to him at the heavy oak table round which such ponderous parish business was conducted. He wondered if Sandy might be able to think of any possible objections to his scheme.

The session clerk had seen no objection. While he contemplated his own features in the polished wood in front of him, the minister had taken swift advantage of the perplexed pause that followed. Considering jocularly that silence gave consent, he ordered Mr Munro to record the motion as passed. He had concluded sweetly with a verse from Ecclesiastes: ' "There is a time to cast away stones and a time to gather stones together." This is the time, gentlemen, to do both.' Then, with a little chuckle, 'At least no one is actually throwing any!'

Now he stepped briskly past the little group of men, and with a cheerful 'Good evening, gentlemen', passed through the kirkyard and up the gravelled lane that led to the manse gates. They stared after his retreating figure in silence.

The manse stood in grounds whose size and stateliness indicated how much closer in origin they were to a lord's country seat than the dwelling place of a humble parish minister. Despite the obvious anomaly, the situation bore no incongruity from one point of view – the Reverend Erskine was entirely lacking in the personal humility which was the badge of his calling, but was far from deficient in the ancient pride of the aristocrat. Thus he belonged to the secular rather than the sacred traditions of the estate.

But for all that, he was not an unpleasant man to know. For his was not a pride which showed itself in haughtiness or vulgarity. On the contrary he was bland and affable in manner, talkative by nature. He was fond of inviting his parishioners to the manse, and was not so ill-bred or so narrow-minded as not to be able and ready to offer them a whole range of expensive wines and cognacs, or liqueurs from bottles that seemed to have come from oriental caves and the shelves of strange apothecaries. The educated in mind or palate were invited to peruse the shelves of the well-stocked library or cellar; over the centuries the grapes of wine and wisdom had been harvested by men of discerning taste in either sphere.

Old ladies drank tea under parasols on the smooth-shaven lawn, and admired the rhododendrons. And he listened to them all, and he listened with genuine understanding and the mildest condescension. It was a condescension which arose from the big frog's acceptance of the tiny pool in which the history of life-cycles had spawned him. He liked to stand in his many-windowed study and look out across the miniature world, feeling himself the spiritual monarch of all he surveyed. His forefathers had ruled their bodies; he, like his more recent ancestors, was the shepherd of their souls. This was the root of his vanity. He was carrying on the ancient family tradition.

His son Robert would carry on that tradition after him. He was in his final year at St Andrews University. The mother had died in her late forties, soon after they had forged together the link in the great chain.

The only unattractive form which the minister's pride often took, was the habit of talking at boring length to buttonholed parishioners about his lineage. Not that there was any questioning its fascination. The Erskines were traceable in Kilrenny as far back as the thirteenth century. One of the family had, in fact, become a Dominican friar, so that the reverend liked to joke with those who understood him, that his pedigree went back to one of the original Domini Canes, the Hounds of God.

There was an unfortunate gap in the family records in the seventeenth century, and his dedicated researches had thrown up nothing relating to this. Then, when the records suddenly resumed, in 1679, the lairds had strangely converted themselves into the spiritual overlords of the community, the house and surrounding grounds going to whichever son would take the cloth. There had been one or two rights of first refusal, but there had never been a breach, and of this he was proud. The tercentenary of the miraculous conversion was due to fall in four years time, the year of his retirement, and he was already planning a grand celebration for the occasion.

Now he stood in his firelit study and looked down at the darkened churchyard. He smiled. Graveyards were for ghouls. And Kilrenny had its share of those macabre old gravestones whose sepulchral gloom and spine-chilling inscriptions were calculated to turn the thoughts of the most life-loving Christian to change and decay. He would change all that.

His was a religion which did not lay its emphasis on worms and epitaphs. The souls of the dead were sooner to be seen in the butterflies that haunted the place in summer, and God whispered to men in the leaves that rustled by quiet waters; his voice was not to be heard in those crude memento moris of earlier times. Before his time was out in Kilrenny, the minister reflected, he might even have the whole kirkyard a landscape garden. Meanwhile, the lily-pond project was under way. His smile grew more benevolent. He poured himself a cherry brandy.

Three months later the session house was gone, and the area it had occupied was sunken and paved, awaiting the water, the flowers and the fishes. There had been no incident to mar the proceedings, as

Gourlay had predicted. No grisly spectre had arisen to protest the sharing of its habitation with living things. Indeed, a happy discovery had been made among the neglected lumber of the session house. It was an old kist, crammed with books, and the minister had it transported into the manse like a coffin on the shoulders of the four workers.

Mostly it was found to contain bible commentaries in Latin, lives of saints and martyrs, some early collections of psalms, books on local history and such like. They were not without interest and one or two were magnificently bound. Despite the foxing, the mildew and the worm holes they represented a collection of considerable value.

But the real prize was the Sexton's Book. This was a massive manuscript volume containing meticulously compiled information on all the early burials carried out by the parish kirk. Details were recorded of names, dates, causes of death, burial sites, inscriptions, memorials and so on. It was written, of course, in the various hands of the sextons of Kilrenny who had seen the generations wither and pass. For hundreds of years they had laid down mattock and spade to record in faded ink the toll taken by death on his parish visits. Then they had lain down themselves and another hand had recorded the fact in a different script and the style of another personality. Some were crabbed and laconic, others wrote flowingly and with garrulous zest. All the entries were difficult to decipher, however, and Mr Erskine looked forward to his summer break when he might have the leisure to examine the book thoroughly. The extant records went back only to the eighteenth century, so that the discovery of this earlier document was an important find for the local church.

On a brilliantly sunny June morning the minister walked down from his manse to watch the pond receive its baptism of water and its first quota of fin and flora.

Lilies whose fate is so often to fester on graves now floated, Ophelia-like, in the shimmering shallows, and fish which had gawped at shoppers from a window-tank in St Andrews now added the glint of gold and the flicker of life to the cemetery's deadness. The reverend's cup was brimming over.

Several times that day he returned to the pond and drank in its beauty and its peace. He noticed that from a distance it caught the sun, and then it would gleam like gold against the grass's emerald.

Standing close by, he could see how it made the church walls flicker with moving veils of reflected light. The water itself was of an astonishing clarity; the living things that lent it colour and movement had been given a lovely home. Wilderness was paradise.

The following afternoon, after lunch, he strolled down to the kirkyard again to watch the sun at work in the water. He was disappointed that the pond had not attracted any local attention, but then this was just its second day.

He passed through the gates which throughout his lifetime had stood in the shadow of the session house. At once he felt the warm flicker of reflected sunlight tickle his right cheek. For a few seconds he stood there contentedly, looking past the pond at the crazy array of stones among which the swallows flitted and the butterflies danced in silence. He would have a seat placed here for talking age and whispering lovers. It would attract them now; the place of tombs had lost its terror. He heaved a long slow sigh of satisfaction and gazed into that fascinating world which his enlightened enterprise had opened up in this fringe of desert.

He gasped. Jerking his hands from his pockets he dropped at once to a crouching position and peered into the water, his face a tense mixture of bewilderment and pain.

The goldfish were dead. Seven large fish had been introduced to the pond on the previous morning. Like living blades they had flashed their suppleness from corner to corner; their bright eyes had been jewels in the hilts of these golden heads. Now seven pale bellies insulted the sky with the dullness of death. Five were on the surface in the middle. Two lurked dismally at the edges of one of the large lily leaves.

It was then that he noticed the second thing. The lilies had started to wither. The petals were quite brownish and the leaves were shrivelling up. The entire picture was one of putrefaction. Except for the water – its clarity and sparkle seemed as unnatural as what had happened to these poor dumb denizens of the pond. How swiftly death had devoured them!

'I must telephone', he whispered. The tautness of his pale features was set off oddly by the dancing light-patterns that played on them.

He stood up sharply.

'The pet shop. And the market garden. Yet how . . .?'

Even as he uttered the words he saw the dark figures walking up to the manse gates. He felt a curious chill in his bones and a darkness in his blood. The local police sergeant and constable were calling to find him out. Death the Skeleton and Time the shadow were at his gates.

The Reverend Charles Erskine never made his telephone calls.

He had never been a man disposed to extra-sensory perceptions of any kind, even religious, and certainly not occult. And he seldom thought of death. Yet he had known, even as he hurried up breathlessly behind the two officers of the law, and beheld their white, awkward expressions, that his son Robert was dead.

The last examination over, five of the students in the theology class had gone out on a small fibre-glass boat which belonged to the uncle of one of them. They had taken with them bottles of beer and the euphoria of release. Naturally they were jubilant. And in perfect summer weather they had quaffed and caroused till death did them part. A lobster fisherman had shouted to them from his small boat a warning which they had neither heeded nor understood. And so they drifted round the coast to Fifeness.

And there those would be skippers of men's souls had foundered on the hidden rocks their inexperience knew nothing of. The lurking teeth crunched into splinters the paperweight world of their craft. Three had made it ashore. Robert and another were non-swimmers. One week later the last of the Erskine line was washed up at Earlsferry.

The funeral was a dismal affair. The Reverend Erskine buried his son beside his mother in the steady rain of early July, just outside the south-east window of the church.

There was a massive turn out. The villagers from several parishes filled the little kirkyard for the service. They stood like black stones among the grey, watching the rain flood the open grave into which the coffin squelched, listening to it hiss into the lily-pond, which no one regarded.

'Earth to earth, ashes to ashes, dust to dust, in sure and certain hope of the resurrection to eternal life through Jesus Christ our Lord.'

The sodden earth thudded down on the coffin lid and the minister walked away through the crowd with streaming face. His hair was plastered over his brow, his right hand thick with clay. The session clerk was at his side.

As they came round to the main doors to go back to the vestry, Mr Erskine paused by the pond, and Sandy waited awkwardly.

'Have it filled in Sandy – not the two who made it, use the other pair. As soon as you can manage.'

The curious fate of the lily-pond had been pushed out of the front page position of local gossip by the drowning tragedy. Naturally there was some speculation. Some of the godless in the community sniggered across their tankards that Gourlay, that narrow-nosed killjoy of the kirk, had come in the night like a stage-murderer with a phial of poison to infect the minister's delight. Others in the congregation whispered over their bibles that the angel of the Lord had stretched out its arm by divine command and shrivelled up this cleric's blasphemy. One or two even surmised, in holy solitude, that God had struck down Robert Erskine for the same, and blasted the tree of the reverend's pride. But no one exchanged that theory with another in pub or pew.

Whatever the reason for the blighting of the pond, Sandy lost no time in acting on the minister's request to have it refilled. The two non-churchmen in his employ were taken from their work up at the manse that afternoon, and ordered to carry out this less sacramental task.

Curiously enough, it was when this was being done that the discovery was made.

The rain had ceased and a fierce sun was lifting the steam from the earth. Mr Erskine was standing at his windows watching the men at work. They had pumped the water over the dyke and into the street, and it had gone sloshing down over the steep brae to fill the ditch behind the grass verge. They had lifted most of the stones from the bed of the short-lived pond, and now they were kneeling down, evidently tired.

The minister was about to turn away when he noticed with surprise that one of the men had started to dig. Now they were both digging. The pond had only been a few feet in depth, and they were fairly hurling spadefuls of soil onto the surrounding grass.

'What are they up to?' he murmured, interested despite what had happened. Then he uttered a little cry of astonishment. They were lifting their spades high in the air and bringing them down with great crashing blows onto the heaps of upturned soil.

'What on earth are they attempting to destroy? Good heavens, I must stop them!'

He ran downstairs and out of the back door, where Sandy was working alone at an ornamental wall.

'Sandy, come quickly!'

And he ran across the lawn to the small side door in the garden wall. The session clerk had never before seen the minister propel himself with anything other than the customary sedateness of a man of the cloth. He stared after his fleeing figure for several seconds, then dropped his mallet and chisel and lumbered in pursuit of him.

The two men arrived at the pond together. The workmen saw them approach and stood up from their destructive efforts. They looked sheepish and awkward.

'Well, what is it?' inquired the minister.

By way of reply they looked down at the debris they had created. Sandy spoke the answer for them all.

'Skeletons.'

The minister's lips parted wordlessly and there was a long silence. The brown heaps on which the workmen had just been venting their fury were flecked with whitened bones, and here and there could be seen the sightless stares of skulls. They lay scattered round the edges of the pit like dumb spectators of their own ignominious exhumation. The reverend counted six skulls in all, some of which had been badly fractured, presumably by the spades.

'And what's the bloody sense in all this?' exploded Sandy, confronting his men. Mr Erskine had never heard him swear. For that matter neither had his workers. They seemed confounded and made no answer. Sandy snatched one of the spades and tossed it aside in a gesture of incomprehension.

'Well? What's the meaning of behaving like lunatics? Do you realise what you're doing, you men?'

'Sandy, it's all right.'

The minister suddenly understood. They had come here to fill in a hole and had been confronted by the ultimate emblems of their own mortality. King Death had grinned out at them from the chambers of the earth, and that ancient smile of recognition had kindled in them a fury and a fear which they had not understood. They had dragged from his lair that obscene tyrant and tried to break him. They had simply been unable to cope.

'I thought', said Sandy, 'that there were no lairs in this part of the kirkyard.'

'I know, Sandy.' The minister spoke quietly and slowly.

'The thing is, these poor people, whoever they were, were never buried in the churchyard in the first place.'

'I don't understand your meaning, minister.'

Sandy sighed and ran a hand through his white mop. He was not in his element here.

'Look, I'll show you.'

The three puzzled men followed the minister down the sloping mound.

Halfway down he stopped in front of a large upright headstone.

'I daresay you've seen this stone hundreds of times, Sandy. But have you ever considered the implications of its inscription?'

All four pairs of eyes converged on the stone. It read:

1810

FIVE FEET NORTH OF THIS STONE

AND EIGHTEEN FEET FROM

THE DYKE

LIE THE BODIES OF JOHN AND SARAH BETT

AND NINE OF THEIR CHILDREN

'Let us carry out the experiment, gentlemen.' The minister showed no obvious signs of any interest in the experiment.

'I've done it before, of course.'

They paced out the stated distance. They were still a good thirty feet from the boundary wall. Three stood there among the stones and waited for the other's explanation.

'That stone was erected in 1810, as you saw. And at that time the dyke was where we are standing now. Look.'

Sandy followed his pointing finger and bent down, parting the blades of grass.

'Sandstone', he pronounced simply.

'The remains of the foundations of the original boundary. The churchyard was extended in 1811, the year after that stone was put up. At some time before 1762, the date the session house was built, these people, whose remains we have just seen, were buried outside the churchyard wall – in unconsecrated ground.'

'But why?'

'That we shall never know', sighed Mr Erskine, returning to the site of the discovery. 'We can postulate a number of likely reasons, of course, but we might have discovered some clue had we unearthed the remains carefully, and not in this – this fashion.' He waved a hand ruefully across the charnel heaps around the pit.

'You had better begin filling everything in again.'

He trudged off heavily.

'Mr Erskine.'

'Yes?'

'There's another one in here yet, I think.'

One of the men was half bent over, peering into the middle of the hole. The minister returned to the scene. A small white rounded protrusion was showing just beneath the edge of one of the last remaining flagstones.

'Lift those stones', he said.

'If you don't mind sir', said Sandy, when the last stones had been removed, 'me and the men'll go back to the manse while you carry out your excavations'.

'Yes, that's all right.' The minister was scarcely hearing him.

'I'll be a while here, I expect.'

He bent down and began to scrape slowly at the soil.

Six hours later darkness had not yet overtaken the minister as he completed his labours. He sat up painfully and leaned against the edge of the pit, contemplating his find.

It was not a complete skeleton. Only a headless, legless torso had been buried there. Where the skull should have been there was a solid block of whinstone. Yet he noticed that the neckbones were all in place. The head had evidently been removed with some care.

The pelvic sockets told the same story. Not a vestige of femur bone was to be seen in them. The right arm was also missing. The left one was slightly bent, and through the elbow had been driven a stone peg, riveting the limb to the side of the pelvic bone. It had taken him half an hour of careful effort to remove this without breaking it.

Between the left upper arm and the rib cage was lodged a single whelk shell, and another lay beside the left hip. He was well aware of their significance. The graveyard was not a raised beach; there had never been any evidence of shell deposits. Clearly the corpse had spent some time in the sea before its interment.

Despite their comparative largeness, the shells might easily have been missed by a less dedicated investigator. But Mr Erskine was a patient man. His thoroughness had even located the coffin nails, still with tiny portions of decayed wood clinging round their heads. Their relative positions confirmed the small size of the box which had contained the truncated remains of a human being.

The skeleton was extremely small-breasted. Pathology was not his particular branch of mortality; he was trained to examine souls and not the bodies which contained them. Still, he would easily have guessed it to be that of a woman.

He rose stiffly to his feet and out of the grave. A stiff breeze was blowing off the sea, from which his position and hours of concentration had sheltered him. He shivered, and as he stretched the muscles of his aching back, noticed the first stars rising out of the darkening firth.

He looked down at the neatly exposed skeletal remains in this strange grave, then at the scattered jungle of bones around its edges. What was certain was that he had just uncovered a witch. And it seemed that an entire family had perished along with her. Probably the other skeletons were complete, but on the body of this poor wretch had been visited the indignities of mutilation after what untold horrors of torture and what weird and watery death?

A thought entered his mind like a shadow. Was this why the lily-pond had...? Was this why Robert...? He thrust it aside, viciously. Why should he put himself into the same category as those superstitious fools who had slaughtered this woman and six others?

'Barbarians!' he exclaimed aloud. His voice sounded unfamiliar in the gathering night.

Then came another shadow, darker than the first. Who could these same ignorant barbarians have been but his own ancestors? After all, the church would have conducted the whole grisly business. But when did all this happen? That was the crucial question. How long before the session house? Before the family conversion? If only those skulls could tell the tale.

'Son of Man, prophesy unto me', he whispered, 'shall these bones live again?'

He bent and picked up the nearest. A cry of anguish escaped him as he saw how small a skull it was, and how tiny were the teeth – milk teeth, obviously; the second set had not yet erupted from the bone. They had killed an infant.

Then he noticed something else – the forehead was not domed as it should be, but seemed to slant backwards with unusual flatness and suddenness. A deformed child, probably mentally retarded. He groaned aloud and clutched the skull tightly for a few moments. Then, trembling, he laid it back gently in the soil. Perhaps it was best after all that in the absence of records this hideous thing would be exposed no further. Yet if only he could be sure.

It was then that he remembered. Records! The sexton's book – it would be there, all the details with the crucial dates. The answer was waiting for him up at the manse. He had to know. He lurched painfully into the dark.

The housekeeper had lit the study fire as usual, but had left long since. Seated by the embers for warmth, with the heavy tome damp across his knees, he started to read the first faint entries.

What a catalogue of human mortalities! It seemed to him as he read that he was reliving all the sufferings of homo sapiens from Adam onwards. It was a depressing crushing task. The pages swam before his eyes and he started to doze off. He seemed to be standing by, a helpless spectator, watching the generations tumble endlessly over death's awful precipice, and he did not know if he was dreaming this or just thinking it.

He jerked himself properly awake, rose and made himself a pot of black coffee. Somehow the domestic articles he handled in the process did not seem real. When he returned to those sombre pages it seemed that they represented all that was truly meaningful. Yet it was so crushingly sordid; the king of terrors did not appear here in pomp and splendour but in all the unthinkable details relating to death and burial, as recorded by an age whose sensibilities were so much coarser than his own.

The reverend grew exhausted, and began to feel as if he were nearing the verge of a nervous collapse. He thought of going to bed and resuming the grim search in the morning.

Even as he thought it a name leaped out of the page at him. A cold hand clutched at his heart. He started to tremble. There in faded brown ink and on paper yellowed with antiquity, the name danced before his eyes. It was his own name. Erskine. He gripped the book firmly and read on.

These were not legal records, of course. The sexton had written down only what seemed to suit his particular taste and the traditions of his time. The bulk of the affair remained undisclosed, locked away in those skulls in that terrible old grave. But there was more

than enough to expose the main facts as mercilessly as the minister
had stripped these last bones of more than three centuries of soil.

In the year sixteen hundred and twenty-six the representatives of
God in the parishes of Kilrenny and Crail were charged by their
ministers to investigate certain charges of damnable sorcery and
devilish practices that had been laid at the very door of the big house
itself, for which many were exceedingly sorrowful. The chief person
suspected of variously reported heinous crimes against God, his
ministers and their children in Kilrenny was Mistress Erskine,
Margaret. She was taken and questioned concerning her dealings
with demons and other abominable instruments of Satan, and under
torture she implicated her two sisters and their husbands and also
her maidservant. She was greatly loth to allow that her youngest
child, Elizabeth, had also been privy to their practices, but the
torturers made her to confess the truth at last concerning this
wretched infant, sometime cursed by God as had been suspected by
reason of those deformities of body and soul manifest in her from
birth. All were properly tried and found guilty of the most hellish
witchcraft.

Mistress Erskine was taken to the Basket Rock off the shore at
Sillerdykes, and there she was pinned down by weights and left to
suffer the washing of two tides, a cleansing of her filthy spirit more
merciful, in consideration of her high place, than the searing pur-
gatory of the stake. Her recovered corpse was dealt with by the
same who had been her questioners, and with the aid of the sexton
in the following manner.

Her legs were removed so that her reanimated corpse might not
stalk the village vengefully after her burial. The right arm, with the
all-powerful pointing finger was dealt with in the like manner, and
the left made fast to her side, that no vampire flight might be
attempted by aid of whatever devils returned to re-enter her
damned corpse. Thus were the limbs restrained from fleeing into
mischief and the hands from wicked acts.

Chiefly to suffer destruction was the head, with its index, the evil
eye, the mischievous and perverted brain, and the cursing tongue.
A whinstone was laid in its place within the coffin, obdurately to
prevent whatever unimaginable entities that haunted the places of
the dead by night from revitalising the spaces wherein such wickedness had been conceived.

Thus unable to see her way, achieve motion by whatever means, curse or blight, or even dream of wickedness – that incomprehens-ible chamber of the mind having been severed from the frame which executed its schemes and fulfilled its designs – she was interred in the unsain ground, without the sanctified boundaries of the kirk-yard, and with her all her fallen crew.

The reverend was nearly bent double with concentration, exhaus-tion, the dim light, and a feeling of hopeless anguish. The conclud-ing pararaph was scarcely visible in the fire's last tired embers. He turned the book to face the grate, and in the red glow imparted to the page he read it aloud.

'Not out of vengefulness or spite, but believing as we do that the evil spirit of this accursed witch would, if permitted, return after sunset and revivify its hellish corpse, roaming the gloomy lanes and glens, and seeking like its infernal master all whom it might devour, we have, in the manner I have described, and with God's own help, aided the ministers of the true Christ against the league of devils in taking these necessary measures, and in the said year of our Lord, sixteen hundred and twenty-six.'

R. S.

The minister shut the volume and sat still in his chair with closed eyes.

So this was his ancestry. Was it better or worse than springing from the misguided peasants who had treated their fellow creatures in such a manner? These and many other questions he revolved round and round in his bewildered brain. How had the others died? There had been no mention of their executions in the sexton's lengthy record. What of the other children in the family, and the laird, her husband. Had he married again? His own family records were silent for more than fifty years after this. And what of the family's decision to enter the church in the succeeding generation? Was it nothing more than a penance? The humility which had made priests out of gentlemen – had it found its origin in nothing more than a mortification of tainted flesh? He would probably never know the answers to these questions. Presumably the family had destroyed a large enough portion of the well kept records to obliter-ate the evidence of their shame. Now he had uncovered the ancient secret to the eyes of the only person to whom it had mattered – himself. But it did not seem to matter much to him now. All that seemed certain to him now was the frailty of all God's family from Adam on.

He rose from his chair and passed to the small windows that faced out to sea. A flash from the May Isle lighthouse broke the darkness and swept across his features. Out there somewhere among the splashing waves was the Basket Rock to which Margaret Erskine had been made fast and left to drown. He thought bitterly of his son.

He put on his hat, his coat and scarf, and walked out of the house.

Back in the churchyard he knelt once more in the grave. It was very dark now, but still his ancestors gleamed at him from their whitened bones. Every terrible detail of what he had read corresponded to the bones that shone beneath the summer stars. As his eyes grew accustomed to the dark he saw again the two whelk shells, where he had left them. The beings that once inhabited these shells had crawled up onto the body of Margaret Erskine, unaware, in their primitive ignorance that they were battening upon a witch. Thus they had been transported from their aimless life of drift with the tides to the finality of this earthen pit – two innocents of the sea to accompany the guilty to an unconsecrated grave.

He put out a hand, meaning to pick them out of their unnatural habitation. Then he withdrew. No, he would leave them where they had lain so long, like the guardians of these bones, the bones of his own lineage that had been so brutally and ironically exposed, strung out upon the city walls of his own pride.

All this would have to be filled in tomorrow, and along with it the Erskine past, and future. He climbed up out of the grave and accidentally put his hand on one of the skulls. He sat on the edge of the grave, picked it up out of its nothingness in the earth, cradled it in his pensive hands. He gazed into its eyeless obscurities.

What thoughts had been contained in these few most mysterious cubic inches of space? What words had played about the vanished lips? He looked up, still clutching the skull. Its eyes had seen those same steadfast constellations – and what else besides? If a man could hold a conversation with a skull, what might he learn?

What more was there to be learned? He threw the skull into the grave, turned, and walked back slowly to his empty manse.

Metamorphosis

ON SUNDAY last I was appointed by the Crail kirk session to take with me three elders, and apprehend on a charge of witchcraft one Janet Morris, daughter to William Morris, farmer at Frithfield, in the parish of Crail; and to bring her before the session for inter-rogation.

It was Jock Fergusson who reported her.

On the Saturday he was coming down past Frithfield on his way to Wormiston, where he kept his creels, and his yawl beached off one of the hinds.

He'd not broken fast that morning, and his throat was as dry as a ditch in June. He remembered the drinking place at the Deil's Neuk, where the water splashed over clear stone. The thought of some of that cold burn gurgling down his gullet was too much for him. He turned aside in his journey.

He was bent over in the act of drinking when he heard her laugh. He looked up, the bowl of his hands brimming with cold sunlight. She was standing there in the burn, not ten yards upstream of him. She hadn't a stitch on.

'Come here, Jock Fergusson', she said.

'I went through the water to her like I was spellbound', said Jock. 'I couldn't take my eyes off her nakedness. The sun was in my face. Her skin was like silver, streaming with water it was, and her nipples were like two wild strawberries a man might pluck on his way to work. Just like two berries after a shower.'

'You desired her, Jock?'

'Aye, God help me, I was under her spell. I would have lain with her but for what happened next.'

'Describe it.'

'She told me to wash her back, in the parts she could not reach. I obeyed, stroking her with hands that trembled. Fire mingled with water as I did so.'

'Did you place your hands elsewhere?'

'Aye.'

'On her private parts?'

'Aye, I put my hand under her flanks and to the front.'

'Well?'

'It was like cupping a rose that has been washed by the rain. I wanted to put my mouth to it.'

'And did you?'

'No. She said "Now you can come up onto the bank with me, Jock Fergusson".'

'And what happened there?'

'That's when I saw what she was really after − to bewitch me. The great oak tree at the Neuk was crowded round with her swine. They were rooting among the fallen acorns, fattening their ugly bellies on the nuts. I was terrified.'

'Go on.'

'She said "Now you can make yourself properly useful".'

'What did she mean by that?'

'October's early enough for acorns. We're three weeks yet before All Saints. She gave me an ashwood club and told me to hurl it up into the branches to bring down a shower of nuts for her beasts.'

'Did you obey?'

'Not me. I was terrified, I told you. I wasn't going to stay in the circle of her swine, and me on my way to sea. I flung the club down and ran off. She was half dressed by this time and came running after me, screaming and shouting.'

'What was it she shouted to you, Jock?'

'She yelled after me that I'd get no lobsters that day, but that the lobsters would feed deep enough on me.'

'Why did you go to sea after that?'

'I'm a poor man. I touched cold iron and hoped for the best. Anyway, I'd encountered the flesh and I thought I'd be ready for the Devil.'

The Devil took Jock in the form of a black northerly that cuffed his small boat angrily out to sea until he'd lost sight of the shore. For five hours he toiled among the huge green castles that were crenellated with foam. He lost all his creels, and nineteen times he thought he and his yawl were going straight to the dungeons, to be shackled in salt. But God and a sturdy tiller brought him home at last, and he told us his tale.

I chose James Leslie, Peter Smith and John Broun to go with me to Frithfield. We rose on Monday morning and set off to carry out our charge.

It was a gray, blustery morning. The sun was a dark frown behind clouds that blackened the sea. Spittings of rain flew at us horizontally and stuck into our hands and faces like splinters of glass. By the time we reached Frithfield we were pierced and chilled to our very bones.

But the worst was to come. From where we stood we could just see our quarry. She was pulling neeps on the shoulder of the hillfield to the east of the house.

Afraid that she would try to give us the slip if she saw us coming, we approached as slyly as we could, our hosen soaked by the shaws and clinging wetly to our legs. We had put on our great black Sunday coats to impress her, but they weighed us down now. There were times we had to crawl through the glaur on hands and knees, as much from tiredness as from not wanting to be seen. We were creatures of mud.

We had got to within a hundred yards of her and still she hadn't seen us. Unhappily, we came on a hurt crow that was lying miserably between the dreels, and he went flapping and croaking away from us and off in her direction, shaking the shaws as he went, and squawking so loud that she turned round.

She half rose, half crouched there on the ridge, a long-haired shadow, ragged against the low sun. But for all that, the devil a scarecrow made she, for that bird made straight for her, a fellow in foulness. Maybe it was one of her familiars, alerting her.

She was still clutching the last neep she ever pulled from her father's field. She stared at us for a few seconds as we huddled there among the wet shaws, looking up at her. Then she flung the neep like a death's head at the carrion thing, and turned and fled.

We could see she was making for the farmhouse. Clearly her guilty soul had trembled when she saw the approach of the representatives of the session.

Now that stealth was pointless we threw off decorum too, and charged. We saw her run into the house, leaving the door open. But she was a lass, and a supple minx, and it was two minutes later that our stiff joints got us there, nearly cracking under the weight of our drenched outercoats. We rushed inside without ceremony.

To our astonishment we found the house to be quite empty and the back door locked and bolted from the inside.

But there – on the kitchen board – lay a black pudding of a monstrous bigness, such as none of us had ever seen. This gigantic thing was more than half the length of the table itself, and as broad as a man's thigh.

This pudding, you will understand, we had reason to believe was none other than the said Janet Morris, who had been converted into such by the Devil, in order to protect her from the righteous wrath of the session.

We looked at it long and hard in silence, then at each other and so back again at the pudding.

Then addressing it, I called out:

'Janet Morris, I command thee in the name of God to reassume thy human shape!'

There was no reply.

Then I said, still addressing it:

'Janet Morris, I apprehend thee on a charge of sorcery and witchcraft, inasmuch as thou didst on Saturday last seek to seduce Jock Fergusson of the Taft Hill, and when he refused to have truck with thee thou didst bewitch him with the aid of devils; and didst raise storms to bring about the destruction of his body, having failed in thine attempt to imperil his soul.'

The infernal thing maintained its impudent silence – a clear sign of guilt. Thereupon I ordered James Leslie and Peter Smith to lay hands on the pudding and carry it back with us to Crail.

Our way was a weary one, such is the weight of sin and guilt, a heaviness that in the normal course of events the righteous are spared. How strangely we were suffered to bear the burden of it! Often we were forced to stop and take turns in the carriage of this monstrosity back to the town.

At long last we reached the Tolbooth, where the keeper, James Fyall secured it, there to await interrogation by the minister.

The pudding was placed in the middle of the great table, and in the full presence of the session the minister repeatedly commanded it to appear in its normal form, which it obstinately and wilfully refused to do, a clear token of its obdurate and guilty fear.

To all the minister's questions as to her dealings with spirits, Janet Morris returned us, in the shape of the pudding, a black, unbroken silence.

Where had she first met with the Devil?

No reply.

Had it been in the Deil's Neuk?

No reply.

Were any of the swine her familiars?

No reply.

To what extent can swine be used in order to bring ill luck on innocent fishermen?

No reply.

Did she confess that she had used them as such that morning, or at least to terrify Jock Fergusson to the extent that he would be hard put to handle the storm which she then raised?

No reply.

The connection with swine was obscenely apparent, but what was the precise demonological significance of her translation into a pudding of black meat?

No reply.

To all our righteous exhortations and entreaties the pudding remained deaf. And throughout all this the shine on its foul skin was the closest thing imaginable to a kind of diabolical gloating in the safety of its own perverse transformation. At one point I could have sworn I saw it smile. If so, that was all we got from it. For the rest, it was a malevolent and blood-congealed silence.

We therefore proceeded to the torture, a slow roasting over the grill in the Tolbooth. James Fyall kept on turning it over with irons while the minister thundered questions at it. All we heard was the smoky crackling of the flames. Then the odour of cooking meat began to assail our nostrils.

Perhaps sensing the intrusion of bodily into spiritual matters, the minister quickly declared there was no more to be done, and that this wretched female was to expire in manifold sin. James Fyall was ordered to burn the hideous thing to ashes and to scatter them to the four winds.

If that had just been the end of it.

Alas, this James Fyall had an idiot son, Davie, who, when his father was making all proper arrangements for the execution, stole the pudding from the Tolbooth and made off with it in secret. He was searched for high and low but could not be found.

Six hours later he reappeared at his father's house, a miserable figure, pale as a candle and twisted with pain. God help him, the demented boy had so gorged himself on this accursed meat to the sickness of his body and God alone knew to what peril of his soul.

There was loud disagreement among the session as to what the significance of this should be. Learned doctors were sent for, and came down at once from the Presbytery at St Andrews, to examine the boy. They spent hours that night splitting the hair of his sin and the danger in which he stood.

It was clearly a diabolical inversion of the parable of the Gadarene demoniac. As the sick man's devils had entered the bodies of the swine in the parable, so Janet Morris, in the substance of swine, had entered poor Davie Fyall. The principal questions were: whether devils had entered him also, and whether the flesh he had consumed was in part human. Was he unwittingly guilty of cannibalism, or the even greater sin of devil-eating, or both? These matters were fruitlessly dissected long into the night.

Finally he was subjected both to a purgative and to the ceremony of exorcism. In this way they expelled from him everything they could!

*

While this whole noisy business was ringing from the lighted session room, a small Dutch trading schooner, the *Yonge Margritta*, stole out of Crail harbour on a quiet two o'clock tide. It was skippered by Jan Doyes, a young captain who had put into Crail on Saturday to shelter from the same storm that had nearly wrecked Jock Fergusson. He was carrying a cargo of preserved meats and German wines. Some thought he'd been seen up at Frithfield asking about livestock.

When asked about this, old William Morris just smiled and shook his head. Years later though, he murmured into his beard about grandchildren in Groningen.

Much later still Jan Doyes' trading prospered and his became a respected name in the East Neuk, especially in Crail. When he finally died, in 1722, he was interred in Crail kirkyard, near to the minister and elders of the previous generation. His wife died three years later, and the captain's brother, Louveres Doyes, brought her over to be buried alongside her husband – as was only natural.

Aere Perennius

MY GRANDMOTHER had been afflicted by asthma since her early twenties, and I never remember her as anything other than as a sufferer, frequently panting for air, and at times having to suck it into her lungs in great drowning gulps.

In her really bad spells she used to use one of these old-fashioned sprays – a little glass phial with a right-angled neck for pointing down the throat, and a hollow rubber ball attached which she squeezed every now and then, spurting the precious droplets of life into her gasping mouth.

When I was five, and without compassion, I would stand and watch this operation with the child's detached curiosity. It made me think of newly caught fish flapping on the pier, their mouths opening and shutting in soundless agony that you could not enter, like the unreality of a silent film.

That was my grandmother – a creature almost out of its element, her frail frame aligned to armchairs, her life a round of house-bound days. She seldom walked even the length of the street. She spent her years at her window, like some gray, faded flower from a world drained of colour. She knew no springs or blossomings – a season-less evergray, framed behind glass, ash-haired, lined and tired, worn out long before her time.

In spite of this I can recall her old house down by the harbour in Cellardyke as one of the happiest of places. It stood only a few yards from the east pier, its scrubbed doorstep on a footing with lichened rocks, its chimney-smoke trading secrets with the sea. Gulls haunted its window ledges like the happy ghosts of sailors come home.

Inside, it carried the sounds of the tides like an ancient shell. When I slept there some nights I used to lie upstairs, awake in the darkness, listening to the hush of waters as they invaded the whorls of my consciousness, and made my sleeping rich and strange. I remember the house's whispering old corners, the big black-leaded grate with shining doors and gleaming knobs, the copper bubbling bleach like a white witch's cauldron. The low, dark-raftered ceilings had little hooks from which hung clusters of kitchen things that shone and smelled – the familiar constellations of my childhood. Rooms opened on rooms as if through endless mirrors.

The winding oak staircase led with polished steps to a loft crammed with fish-nets, forest-green glass floats, corks, and old sea-boots and sou'-westers in which I'd dress up and go to sea. That loft was my wheelhouse, its tiny skylight my porthole, opening on cloud-fluffed skies that were the foam of perilous seas. And I sat there through eternal afternoons, among broken herring-baskets and lobster-creels that carried the deeps within them like ghosts: they crept through the ancient wicker-work and meshes, and up the nostrils and into the chambers of the ear. Everywhere there lingered the strange smells of old tradition, the salty scents of seafaring legend.

Most vividly of all I remember the evenings. The grown-ups sat round the fire and talked of local characters long dead, whose famous exploits seemed, in my seagreen eyes, to rival those of Viking men and buccaneers.

My grandfather was a fisherman. As he lay back in his fireside chair, rolling cigarettes and talking of Norway and Iceland and the Dardanelles of his wartime days, he seemed to me Odysseus back at his hearth, staring into the embers with china-blue eyes, in which were carried the lure and lore of many horizons.

After he was dead, those who were left sat round the same fire and spoke of his other voyagings, round all those fishermen's pubs, at whose bars he had kept stormy vigil, as at many a helm, until whole seas over and drowned to the world. Mermaids, who all night long had served him Neptune's nectar, bore him homewards at last on their ample breasts. Young hearty uncles laughed at this and slapped their knees, shaking their Brylcreemed heads. Old frail aunts cackled and nodded with sombre restraint, as if afraid to crack open or offend the dead. I remember their faces glowing in the firelight. It was a happy place. Its windows glittered on the sea.

But the young hearty ones married and moved away. And the old dried aunts withered on their stalks, drooped, and fell to earth. And at last my grandmother was left alone.

It was then that the closing orders came. No fewer than twenty-eight souls in Cellardyke woke up one morning to find themselves condemned. They were astonished to see, sliding through their letter-boxes, orders of closure on their homes from the local council. My grandmother was one of the victims. She had never heard of a closing order, and half believing herself to be a kind of criminal, she telephoned me for help. By this time I was working in Edinburgh. I waited until the weekend and drove through to Fife.

It was all viciously simple. Sitting on her doorstep in the sun, beneath a gull-torn sky, I removed from its buff envelope a stiff, folded document headed 'Closing Order'. This is how it read:

> The local authority is satisfied that the above dwelling-place does not reach the standard deemed tolerable by the 1977 Scotland Housing Act, and that it ought to be demolished. The authority prohibits the use of the house for human habitation as from twenty-eight days from the date on which the closing order becomes operative.

There followed a list of the abominations of No. 2 East Shore – its low ceilings, its small windows, its steep, dark stairs, its outside toilet. And it went on to say that if these defects were rectified within twenty-eight days, the order of closure would be lifted. Otherwise legal proceedings would start. The alternative was to accept the purchase of the house by the council and to move into a modern rented house on the large new scheme just completed up by the main road. This fearful assault, and battery of words was signed by Albert Mansini, Chairman of the Housing Committee.

Mr Mansini's family had made their money selling ice-cream in Kirkcaldy. Mr Mansini had ploughed the profits into boat-building, coming to Cellardyke and taking over the small local shipyard after its owner died. But the tide of business had long gone out, and the councillor would have been stranded high and dry but for the fact that he had a second source of income, and one that never failed. He was the local undertaker. All year round Mr Mansini built his ships of death and launched them on the kirkyard's green wave, to carry embarking villagers like Vikings to their final haven.

That at least was the way he liked to see it, for he fairly warmed to his chilly theme. He prided himself on providing a smooth passage to eternity. At funerals, when relatives were caught in sudden squalls of grief, he was a picture of unruffled calm. From the laying out to the shipping in he took care that all went well. The merest details of coffin cards and cords were not overlooked by his watchful weather-eye; he had them all charted. He was death's draughtsman and master-navigator, a true professional on whom a dead man could depend.

But Mr Mansini suffered from the besetting sin of middle age –

the greed for gold. Corpses rattled like coins into their graves, and coffins were laid like ingots beneath the ground. Grasping for grave-gold as my grandmother had gasped for air – that was the man who, as Housing Chairman, had recently employed a smart young London architect to design the council's new scheme, and had designated as sub-standard twenty-eight of the oldest houses in the village. There were thirty houses in the modern scheme.

I called that morning at his own bright bungalow on the braehead. The door was opened by his poisonous wife Agnes. She fixed me with eyes like hat-pins, nippily informing me that her husband was at the town hall seeing the burgh surveyor on very important business. 'In connection with the closing orders', she sneered. She remembered me, and doubtless wondered if anything good could come out of Cellardyke – or back to it. I showed her my back and made for the town hall.

Mr Mansini was just slipping out and wanted to get down to his office at the boatyard. Then at two o'clock he had a funeral. He was, he told me busily, hard-pressed this morning, and I should have to walk along. I had no option but to dance attendance at his side. He was short and palely plump and padded along like a sleek fat fox.

I began by asking him if he had ever actually set foot in No 2 East Shore.

'That's not necessary sir', he replied formally, 'seeing everything is in the plans'.

'But if you actually stepped inside the house I'm pretty sure you'd agree it's a very fine old dwelling-place.'

'That may be, but it's antiquated. Mrs Scott's house is like every other one down by the east pier. Windows too small, skylights needing enlarged, ceilings too low. Not nearly enough natural light getting into them.'

'But according to your closing order', I protested, 'even that magnificent old staircase has to go. What's wrong with it?'

'Too steep by far, and excluding too much light. It should be replaced by a Ramsay ladder – you know, one of these collapsible aluminium ones.'

'But my grandmother would never negotiate one of these affairs. Besides, that staircase is made of solid oak.'

'Oh, I'd find a use for the oak.' One of his eyes almost twinkled. 'In any case Mrs Scott would be much better off in one of our new houses, especially in her state of health. Why don't you persuade her to accept a modest sum for it and move into the scheme – if you really want to do her a good turn?'

'You might as well place a closing order on her life', I said bitterly. 'It strikes me you're a lot less interested in my grandmother's well-being than in profiteering for the council, not to mention yourself!'

To my surprise he turned contemplative rather than nasty. By this time we had reached the top of the brae commanding a view of his twin professional preoccupations, boatyard and kirkyard. His eyes merged with the shimmering sea, and his voice became a far-off hum, as if his thoughts were spiralling out of some mysterious shell.

There was a time, he reflected, when mud huts had sufficed for the living while massive monuments were erected for the dead, and stone had been turned into tombs long before it had ever been used for houses. In his time he had had a lot to do with building for those on both sides of the grave, but he prided himself on not discriminating between the two. Many old salts, now lying in the cool and comfort of the old kirkyard, had endured living conditions that were nowadays intolerable. As for mansions in the sky, these were the minister's business. But as housing chairman and undertaker he was concerned with more immediate problems of accommodation.

'Still, no reason not to build well', he concluded. '*Aere perennius.*' His Latin startled me. 'Monuments more lasting than bronze.'

And without further comment, the poetics of his profession firmly established, he turned and trotted sedately down the brae. He seemed oddly untouchable.

I stared after him, that macabre monologue of his sounding strangely in my ears. Each of his words glittered like nails in the life of the village. Beneath me the red-tiled roofs of all the old fisher houses spilled happily towards the harbour. Systematically, he and his like were hammering at their roots, severing them from their links with the ancestral sea. Foreigners and the rootless rich would crawl into them like crabs for a short season; then they would scuttle off aimlessly, the scavengers, leaving the houses like varnished shells, formally, lifelessly pretty. The sea no longer sung in them the tunes of the old times. They became like history without legend, literature without poetry, flowers which had lost their perfume.

In the next few weeks, without any assurances of legal incompetence on the part of the council, and with her anxiety over the issue

producing alarming effects on her precarious health, my grandmother decided to capitulate.

And so the old lady was invalided into one of the smart new
homes and into the brave new world of mod cons. The week after
she was installed I drove through from Edinburgh to see her new
house.

It was a monument to tastelessness.

The rooms had the dimensions and colours of an ice-cream seller's van, and that much atmosphere. The whirring electric fire that
spun no dreams, the storage heaters she could not afford to burn,
the stainless steel sink unit that was too high for her, and the
avocado toilet-suite she had to toil upstairs to use – these were
what were intended to help her live with some dignity.

But to the spirit the place was antiseptic. Her past did not exist
here. The ghosts that had peopled her old cottage like a mellow
feeling, a winy diaphanous haze lingering about the place – they
did not follow her up the brae to her new house. She lived from then
on in a vacuum.

And in a vacuum she died, finally, five months later – two days
after a gray Christmas.

A neighbour moved into the house to help with the funeral
arrangements. The coffin was brought up to the bedroom where she
was laid out, and some old acquaintances arrived in a black, straggling line to look their last. She was buried on the last day of the
year. The funeral party gathered downstairs in front of the electric
fire with its plastic coals that barely sufficed to take the chill off the
bleak December day.

When the minister had finished his prayers six of us filed upstairs
in slow motion to bring the coffin down and stow it into the waiting
hearse. We were directed by Mr Mansini himself.

But a strange reversal occurred. As soon as we lifted the coffin
from its trestle and moved with it to the bedroom door, it was clear
that the space between doorway, house-wall and stairhead simply
did not provide enough turning room to manoeuvre the coffin into a
position that would enable it to be lifted downstairs. We stood
there, frozen.

'Come back – backwards', whispered Mr Mansini. We retreated
and stood there awaiting further orders, moveless as a medieval
sculpture, a cortege cast in black bronze. The coffin was beginning
to feel that way.

The undertaker's eyes darted impatiently.

'Look, lay the box down again, and two of you try it this time. You take the head', he said to me. 'James', – to his assistant – 'take the feet'.

The two of us attempted what the six had failed to do. It was no use. The coffin's shining solidity seemed to fill up the entire room. Its uncompromising bulk was making the two of us totter and sweat.

'It's academic, Mr Mansini', I breathed.

'Eh?' He glowered at me, wrinkling his nose in disgust. The minister's anxious footfall was heard on the stair.

'Ah. Just a little question of space, Mr Robertson. Don't worry, we'll have her out of here in no time at all.' The undertaker coughed loudly and took over my end of the burden. He and his assistant struggled to force it the way it had to go. Plaster flew from the wall as Mr Mansini began to behave rather like a bull.

When the minister saw how they were trying to manoeuvre this malevolent-seeming mass, he interrupted them at once.

'Gentlemen, this is all to no avail! There's only one way to do it – you'll have to stand the coffin on end and walk her round to the stairhead. And judging by the steepness of these stairs you'd be well advised to walk her all the way down as well. That's obviously the way the coffin came in.'

'But Mr Robertson, it's hardly the way a body should go out!' The undertaker was shocked.

'Oh, come now, Mr Mansini. If Mrs Scott suffered such cramped conditions while she was alive, she's scarcely going to object to the same indignities in death.'

At the minister's irony the other man's face turned bright red. But he could see that there was just the one way. They turned the coffin up on its end and walked my grandmother downstairs, a step at a time.

'Dinna cowp it, dinna cowp it!' hissed Mr Mansini, lapsing into Scots in his terror. The minister made a face and followed them. The six of us then trooped downstairs and reassumed our positions as pallbearers.

We stepped out into the street that was just receiving the bitter benediction of the first winter snow. A black colony of ex-fishermen lined the pavement opposite, brave old penguins standing to attention in the rising wind. Not one of them, nor anyone peering from behind curtained windows, would have guessed that all had not gone according to tradition within the new house.

But the undertaker was not allowed to forget the matter. As the hearse moved off, purring like a black cat among the falling flakes, the old men reverently removed their hats and clapped them to their chests. Bald and blue-veined pates were bared a moment to the freezing skies, then they quickly clapped them on again and fell into line behind us. Mr Mansini walked to the right of the hearse, his assistant to the left.

Suddenly one of the pallbearers, an old fisherman who had worked with my grandfather, raised his voice like a gentle prophet in the mourning wind. Shaking his head, he jabbed a thumb at the housing scheme that we were leaving behind, and lamented the passing of the old order in a single telling sentence.

'Eh, Mr Mansini', he sighed, 'thae hooses werena made for daith!'

The undertaker stopped in his tracks, stunned by the double insult that had been so neatly dealt, and with such unintentional irony, to his two life's concerns. His clever young London architect from the urban world of funeral parlours and crematoriums had overlooked the simple fact that houses were died in as well as lived in, and that up here at least, certain traditions also died a hard death. The procession moved on without him, following the hearse at its slow, relentless pace.

Looking back, I saw him still standing there, open-mouthed. He was staring at the housing scheme as if seeing it in a new light. His figure was whitening fast as he stood. Perhaps he would remain there forever, I thought, turned to snow as a sort of penitential monument to his own disgrace, a weeper, mourning the folly of the times.

But as we came within sight of the snow-caped church, by the chilly, glinting sea, I knew of course that he would be there. I knew that when we reached the graveside, and buried my grandmother in the broken white bread of the earth, that he would be there all right, chastened and subdued maybe, but there – ready in some small funereal way, perhaps, to make atonement to my grandmother's lingering spirit, for his most unprofessional treatment.

Earth's Highest Station

ROB DIED in 1961, having just reached the age of eighty.

I was in my final year at school at the time and I went down to see him the day before he died. I was glad I had done that. Not because I didn't visit him often enough – I used to drop in quite a bit after school and take a late bus home to St Monans. And it was not because he had told me the story – on that last day before his old heart suddenly stopped beating. That was not why I was glad to have been there. After all, he told me the story nearly every time I went to see him. It was one of the few sunny spots left to him in life, and I liked to listen to it for that reason alone. It was like an old photograph that a man keeps taking out of his wallet over and over. In time it became worn, but never a detail of it changed, because it was taken from life.

I was glad I had seen old Rob, simply because I was the last soul he had talked with, and the last to hear his well worn story. Rob's own version had been passed on to him from first hand, and to get it from Rob just before he died – well, that was a little like being handed an embered brand and asked to blow it back into life.

That's what I want to do now.

It was a brilliant afternoon in June.

I came out of school and made my way along the High Road to Cellardyke harbour, clutching a bagful of English and History textbooks. Rob's cottage at the harbour head stood steeped in sunshine and silence, its whitewashed walls thrusting back the blue and gold shimmer of sun and sea I stooped through the open door and stepped into the kitchen on the seaward side of the house. Rob was sitting in a pool of sunlight that made the scrubbed flagstones twinkle.

'Hello Rob', I said.

He looked up from his far-off scrutiny of the floor. His old eyes brightened.

'Och, it's you lad. Come away in. Come round to the fire with you. The kettle's on.'

Summer or winter, Rob never let that fire go out. He kept it burning all night, raked out the white dross in the morning, and placed new coals over the last night's embers. The fire was the crimson heart of his house that beat from red to white and back again throughout the quiet seasons and the winter storms. It never stopped until he did.

He rose from his chair, and I was aware of the black waterfall of his trousers, the threadbare raggedness of his navy blue guernsey that had shrunk in a thousand washes.

'Will you take a cup of tea?'

He waved me to one side of the hearth and bent over the grate with the tongs to take the kettle off the coals. It was a great black songster, sooty with age and the fires of his ancestors. Uncountable cups that cheer had warbled inside it throughout many lifetimes, and passed singing into bloodstreams long run dry.

He sat down opposite me, the sunlight bathing his gray head and picking out the silver stubble on his chin, making it glisten.

We supped our tea.

'You'll be sitting your Highers then', Rob said.

'Yes', I said. 'History's at the end of the week. I've just sat English.'

'So it'll be off to university with you quite soon?'

'That's right', I said. 'In St Andrews.'

A gull winged its way past the window, a white flash against the blue. It carried across the harbour its long, unbroken laugh, raucous, strident. Perhaps, I thought, it found my university aspirations hilariously irrelevant in this arena of the sea.

'Aye', Rob said, 'it's changed days since I was a boy. Off to sea at fourteen, like my father before me. And my grandfather and his father. And his father before him.'

His eyes drifted to the fireside.

'And that last seaman was the greatest sailor of them all.'

'Thomas Watson', I said.

'Thomas Watson', said Rob. 'My great great grandfather. Bosun gunner on HMS *Victory* at the Battle of Trafalgar, 1805.'

His eyes were lost in the embers now, pale blue draining into red. I drained my cup and set it down in the fireplace. On each side of the grate was what could have been taken for a shot-putt. I knew them to be a pair of cannonballs, more than a century and a half old. I also knew where they had come from. They had been black-leaded so many times, and were so symmetrically placed, that they looked like a decorative part of the fittings in the grate.

I picked up the one nearest to me, as I had done often enough before.

'A thirty-two pounder', Rob said, filling his pipe in preparation for telling his yarn. 'A French cannonshot, fired into the *Victory* from the *Redoutable*, and the biggest shot that came from her that day.'

He nodded his head.

'But it was just a wee musket ball that did the worst damage of all.'

The cannonballs had been passed down through four generations, to lie here with quiet respectability, reflecting the glow from Rob's uneventful kitchen. But I knew that the old man's ancestral link with Trafalgar went deeper and much closer than dead men and silent shot.

'Fancy you speaking to someone who was actually at that battle all these years ago', I said. 'And now here's me speaking to you.'

This was the cue that allowed Rob to happen on his tale.

'Aye', he said. 'Time's short enough when you think about it.'

I thought about it while he struck a match and puffed. A pall of blue tobacco smoke hung round his head for several seconds. Most of it drifted up to the dark beams. Some wisps were sucked away up the chimney by the draught from the fire.

'But just you remember now', Rob went on. 'Thomas Watson's daughter – that was Margaret Watson – she was with her folks during the battle on board the *Victory*. But she was only four and a half years old at the time. She was over ninety when she died. That was in 1892. I was a lad of twelve then, and so I had all her recollections at first hand. And let me tell you, that woman had some memory!'

'I suppose the sort of things she saw would be difficult to forget', I said.

'Well that's true', said Rob. 'But apart from that she remembered every detail of what her folks had told her about their own experiences. And that's half the story.'

'I wish I had a memory like that, Rob, especially with this Higher History coming up.'

The bowl of the old man's pipe winked and gleamed and the blue fumes drifted across the space between us.

'I've forgotten the bulk of that story already', I said at last. 'Do you think you could remind me of some of the details?'

'I'll be glad to. Have some more tea.'

The blackbird sang amid the hearth's autumn fires. The teapot was filled again, and I drank and drank.

'Here', said Rob, 'is Thomas Watson's account of his own adventures. He told it to his daughter and she told it to me. And now I'm telling you.'

THOMAS WATSON'S ACCOUNT OF HIS OWN STORY
1797-1801

I'd had a bad day's fishing. There was no doubt about that.

It was a quiet sea for late harvest, but that was just it. Nothing seemed to be happening, either on high or in the great deeps. All the long day the sun crept like a snail across the sky, sticking very close to the horizon and leaving a thin gray trail of light behind it. My lines went down empty and came up empty, over and over. Nothing seemed real.

I stayed out longer than I should have done, hoping for a catch. When I brought the boat in past Craw Skellie it was so dark I had to steer by memory.

I toiled up the East Green with just a handful of haddocks to show for a dawn to dusk shift on the waves. I could see Mary's face at the window, looking as white as I felt. I held out the haddocks and shook them at her sadly like a bunch of dumb silver bells.

I could hardly believe what I saw next. I saw her mouth open and her head wrench back, and she screamed my name so loud it's a wonder the roof didn't lift clean off the cottage. The next second the door flew open and a body of men sprayed out blue and white like a bursting wave. I didn't wait around to inspect their foreign looking gear. It was as plain as the nose on your face they were the press gang. I hurled the haddocks at the house and fled.

I suppose it was because I was at the top of the brae that I turned by instinct to run back down. It was a stupid thing to do because in less than thirty seconds I was back among the skellies with nowhere to take to but the broad sea.

I ran west along the shore for a minute, making good ground. The sailor boys were at home on the rolling deck no doubt, but I could skim over the bouldered beach like a seagull, my feet scarcely touching the land. When I dropped behind the big skellie I cut up sharply into East Anstruther.

I doubled back then as fast as I could, hoping that the fisher houses would hide me. I was making for my own house. I had to see

Mary, whatever happened. But they had spotted my ploy and came surging up Johnson's Close from the sea, just like the surf does in winter. They were now at my heels and hadn't run as far or as fast.

But as I burst out into the open at the harbour I saw help at hand. Mary had headed a gang of lasses down to the beach. They'd filled their aprons with stones and shingle and were now standing at the bulwark waiting for the tars. As soon as I saw Mary I slowed down and started for her.

'Dinna mind me, you daft loon!' she screamed at me. 'It's you they're after!'

I stood there and looked at her.

'Run!' she screamed at me again. And she hurled me from her.

I flashed past her like a bird, swallowing hard on a lump of words.

'Let them have it, lassies!'

At the sound of my wife's voice I flicked my head round. I saw the pack of sailor boys explode like grapeshot. They stopped and staggered, as if a boat had just jarred on a reef and the crew gone flying into the foam. As I paced along the Mill Road making for the fields I could just hear their bloodied cries sounding crimson in the dark night, and the shrill silver skirling of the women.

When I passed the old kirkyard at Kilrenny, I envied the dead their frozen sleep, life's fitful fever over for them at last. Yet it seemed to me they braced themselves in their graves, cheering me on in a thrill of silent sympathy for my flight.

I made my way up to the Commontry, and so north over the muirs to Kippo, where I slept in the wooded uplands overnight. When the sun bled through at dawn, wounding the sky, I got up cold and sore. I looked down towards the sea. In the morning's red carnage I saw there what I had expected to see – the grim hulk of an English guard vessel, anchored off St Andrews. There could be no question of going back home, not while the press gang were anywhere to be seen in the firth.

I stayed on in Kippo for three days and nights, with nothing to eat but some late brambleberries. It couldn't have been colder or wetter for Jonah in the whale's belly. On the second night October gales ripped through the woods, stripping the last leaves from the trees and making their timbers creak.

The third night brought the rain, flying like arrows on the wind. It started off lightly, flicking its fiery whiplashes about my face, stinging me out of sleep. Then, as the wind died off, it grew heavier, dropping over the woods in a cold, wet curtain. It unfolded itself over me as I lay there among the leaves, a coverlet of chill, solid water.

In the bleak hour before dawn, things froze up, and I knew I had to move or die. But the English sail was still scarring the Forth. I turned my back on the sea and moved inland.

I was out there for another six days – nine days and nights altogether, till the whins of Kingsmuir were as well known to me as the rocks I had waded among since I was a boy. Out there in the country I heard that they had taken horses and were scouring the farms. They were bribing every herdboy on every hillside with English gold.

I kept on the move and by noon on the ninth day I found myself as far off as Airdrie estate. It was there that it came on me to ask for help from the laird. I had sent fish up there from time to time and I had met Sir Andrew once or twice. He spoke like a man whose backside touched nothing but velvet. But for all that I had served him, and he was a countryman of mine.

When I got to the big house I saw a hunting party just new back from their morning's capers. They were red in the face and laughing. Taking courage from their high spirits I went right up among them as they clattered round the back of the house. No one was much interested in me, but I spoke hard to a lackey to ask at the door for me, giving my name.

I waited there so long that I was just on the point of leaving. But to my surprise a man appeared and asked me very politely to follow him round to the front of the house and be admitted like a gentleman. I did just that, thinking to myself that Sir Andrew must have dined well off my choicest fish.

We arrived, through a maze of stairs and galleries and glowering portraits, at a pair of heavy oak doors, which the attendant opened with a slight knock, stepping at once to one side.

'Mr Thomas Watson, your lordship', he announced.

Looking past the old servant, I recognised his lordship sunk deep into a massive chair, the colour of elderberry wine. He was still in his hunting gear. One booted leg was slung slackly over the arm of the chair, and in one hand he flourished a glass. His other arm rose in a sweeping movement as if he was sowing corn. I went in and the doors were closed behind me.

It was when I heard the key click in the lock that I became aware of the presence of the other man in the room. He was standing to the side, silhouetted against a huge window. The noonday sun was streaming past him and into my eyes. He was just a tall black shape.

'Thomas.'

His lordship spoke in his usual drawling tones, but his voice was almost friendly.

'Damned good of you to call, Thomas', he said. 'Would you believe it, I was just going to send for you!'

He laughed redly, threw his pot of gold down his throat, and stood up.

'Thomas', he said, 'I want you to meet Lieutenant Brand – of His Majesty's navy.'

Then he said: 'And Lieutenant Brand, I believe, has been very anxious to meet you'.

As Sir Andrew went off into another laugh, the shape moved out of the sunlight a little, and I caught a glimpse of buttons and braid before I was through the window in a spray of broken glass and sunlight. I picked myself up, spitting out curses and blood against their lordships that would do anything for king or coin.

If they'd used the horses I'd have been theirs, but I prevented that by going through the trees. In ten minutes I was nearly two miles away from the house. I went west again, to Lingo, three miles north of Pittenweem, where I lay in a copse till dark.

But I couldn't spend another night under the sky, and I needed food badly. My feet were swollen with cold and tiredness. So it was that I fixed on returning to Cellardyke. I wouldn't go home, I decided, but to my cousin's house in the East Green. I could lie snug and warm in the closeness of her loft until the press gang finally left the area. There was a full moon but I made up my mind it would be as useful to me as to my trackers. I trudged east again, coming down to the shore when I came in sight of Anstruther.

I crept like a fox along the high road, looking down hard over the roofs. There wasn't a breath of wind. The moon lay in the harbour like a cold gold galleon. There wasn't a sight or sound of life. I threw away nine days and nights of care and ran madly down to my cousin's dwelling.

I was just lifting my fingers to rap on the door when I heard the noises behind me. Before I could turn I was in a circle of hands. I roared like a bull. A bright wave surged through my head and I felt myself lifted off my feet. From under a black sea I could hear my cousin's voice from her top window demanding to know what was happening.

'Keep your Scotch breath to cool your Scotch kail!'

That was the last thing I heard. Then I sank to the bottom of that black sea.

When I surfaced the first thing I saw was Mary's face. She was holding my head in her hands in a dark place. I fought for my tongue and found it.

'Surely to God I didn't get clear of them again? How did that happen?'

'It didn't', she said. 'They took you and I came after them. They wouldn't take me along at first, but they soon saw that there was reason enough for that. We're below decks on HMS *Triumphant*. I think we're on our way to Leith. You ken well where it will be after that.'

I slipped back under the waves of sleep.

She was a nurse, you see. When she told them that, they didn't need much persuasion to take her along. They let her come with me. She served with me at sea for nearly nine years.

To begin with I can tell you I didn't take too kindly to lending my fisherman's hand to the British war effort. But I came to respect their seamanship as much as they quickly recognised mine, and in three years they made a fighter out of a fisher.

The century turned, like a great tide, and carried me high, to the position of bosun gunner on HMS *Ardent*, a line-of-battle ship. She was only a third-rater, mind you, with seventy-four guns. But she was a great fighter, with a scarred and battered old frame. I've a special love for that ship, because that was where my little Margaret was born. Below the decks, in a cabin of that ship, she was born while the guns were thundering.

That was during the battle of Copenhagen in 1801. The Danes had made the shore defences in the Kategat impregnable, so we thought; and it was while our guns were exchanging flaming red ruin with their batteries at Cronenberg that my Mary told me she thought she would deliver that day.

It was just gone half past nine in the morning and three of our ships had already grounded among the shoals. That left nine of us to continue the action, including the *Ardent*. I was in charge of my gun crew when Mary told me the news that our baby was surely coming. I don't know how I got them to shoot straight after that.

She had more nerve than me, as it happened. She continued by the side of the ship's surgeon, binding and bathing, until her own pains were so bad she could no longer stand. And she was sore needed that day. Many a poor sailor's life was cut short, or sadly altered, by the Danish fire. In all my nine years in the navy I never saw such a rain of shot as I saw during that bombardment. Those land batteries were like the teeth of hell. 'Close up, there! Close up!' I seemed to be bellowing all morning, as men fell mangled about my feet, and the spaces they left had to be filled. In two hours the crew were reduced to a surgeon's exhibition of half-formed and three-quarters formed creatures, hardly men at all. Lost heads and lopped limbs and crushed entrails lay all around, and the timbers of the ship shrieked so loud when the ball came tearing through, sending the splinter-swords everywhere – shearing through eyes and throats and groins.

And among all that death-ridden bedlam, down in the cockpit – the bloody womb of the ship – my daughter was born. She was delivered among the dead and dying. One minute Mary was tending to the needs of wounded sailors; the next minute these same men were helping the surgeon bring her baby into the world.

What a birth that was! Her cradle was a rolling man-o'-war that shivered and shook in the North Sea. Her lullaby was the thunder of cannon, the rending beams, the shrieks of mutilated men. And I thought it pitiful and strange that the poor infant's birth-place was the howling centre of such a deadly storm – instead of the quiet back bedroom of our Cellardyke cottage, where the sea made its quiet patterns on the walls.

But it must have been stranger still for all those suffering and doomed beings whose cries were filling the ship, to hear the wail of a new-born babe rise thinly on the air; to see an innocent girl come like that into the world of terrors that they were leaving.

Things looked so bad for us, in fact, that Parker signalled to Nelson in the *Elephant* to leave off. We could see the message clear enough ourselves. But Nelson just took us even closer in. What with all that smoke hanging over the surface of the sea, it would have taken a man with both eyes in his head to make out a message. Or so he said.

Well, Nelson was in a better position than Parker to tell how things might go, and his decision paid off. By half-past two we'd annihilated them.

And after five hours of desperate fighting, I went down to see my wife and child. I was grimy with gunpowder and black with smoke and spattered with blood. I'd seen death grinning at me all morning from a thousand iron mouths. He had screamed at me through the gunports, turning my crew to red wreckage. I could hardly hear or stand, and my nerves hung in scarlet shreds.

But I can tell you, I never felt fear like it when I first set eyes on my newly born daughter, lying on her mother's breast. She was so pink and tiny, this battle-born baby, so completely naked to the death-dealing dangers that had surrounded her. I felt terrified to have brought her into the world. I hadn't dropped any tears for fallen friends, but I stopped to shed them now for that innocent head that was even now receiving the world's baptism of brine and blood.

My employers, who took me so roughly, would have let us all go after that. But strange as it may seem, we stayed in service for another five years, until six months after Trafalgar. And it was more than one bloody sea-battle we came through unharmed before that day in 1805. I can't explain why things worked out the way they did. I suppose I must have caught a taste for adventure, added to my life-long love of the sea.

Rob's pipe-smoke hung in clouds among slanted shafts of sunlight, and for a time his low-roofed cottage was like a scene below the decks of one of these old ships-of-the-line.

'That sea-born bairn was my great grandmother', he said. 'These days it's hard to credit that a bairn could be born under such conditions. Stranger still that she should have been brought up at sea among the same sort of perils. But there's her father's story. She told it to me as he told it to her; and I'll tell you hers as she told it to me.'

The sun swung round the seaward side of the house, and the firth darkened as Rob puffed his way into the second part of his story.

MARGARET WATSON'S ACCOUNT OF HER OWN STORY
1801-1805

My earliest memories are of ships and men.

At first I thought the world was not above a hundred and fifty feet long and forty feet broad. It swam about in a blue waste that was sometimes neutral to us and often made to destroy us. When it moved in our favour the world had a good feel to it.

The human race was not much more than five hundred, and apart from my mother they were all men. They smelled of salt and sweat, and of all the other things that were part of the world they helped to steer – timber and pitch and hemp. My father had a different smell that came from the big guns.

They shouted at each other much of the time too, and often struck one another. But they talked differently to me. Especially the men who wore the heavy clothes with the gold markings. Sometimes one of them would give me sugar or lemonade, and tell me stories of people and places who were far away from where we were, and that I might see one day.

My mother too told me about my real home. It was on the land, she said, but near to the sea, which one day we would stop sailing on and return to our own harbour. That was where we belonged, she said.

Mother had to look after the men when they were hurt.

At first those times frightened me. I knew when all the great white sails appeared between the sea and the sky, that I would be taken down to the dark place near the bottom of the ship – away from my father. I had to wait there until the world stopped its shaking and its rolling, and until all the shouting and the thunder stopped. I had to cover my ears because of the noise.

The first time ever I can remember that happening, a man was running down below with me, holding my hand, and the air about us sang its iron song.

One minute we were running hand in hand. The next, all I can remember is looking at him lying there, still holding my hand. I couldn't see his head. He seemed to have tucked it out of sight beneath a bright red scarf. He was crushing my hand so hard that I tore myself away from him and ran crying for my father. Men tried to catch me, but I slipped under their arms and didn't stop until I found my father, shouting his chorus to the iron songs of the great guns. He crawled away with me among flashes of fire and puffs of smoke; and the bursting of the timbers and the roaring and rolling of the big black cannon were all around us.

We reached the cockpit, where I was always sent.

He shouted to my mother: 'Take this bairn, for God's sake, Mary!' Then he left us quickly. When I looked around me from my mother's arms, warm in the darkness, I saw the poor men who had danced and sung the night before, lying huddled in red, their tongues still now in their pale mouths; or making the noises I had heard pigs and sheep make before we started a voyage.

I watched my mother then, moving about among the remains of men, lifting them with her strong arms that were crimson-gloved to the elbows, helping to hold them down while the man with the shining blades did awful things. I wondered if I should have to do the same as my mother when I grew to be her size.

After a time I grew used to the battles, though I never liked them. I liked the times best when I sat on my father's knee while he jigged me up and down in time to the songs that the sailors sometimes sang. Or when my mother gave me sweet things, and held me close in bad weather. Or the times when I could look up and see all our sails racing like the clouds across the blue sky, and the masts bending, and the ship going up and down in a creamy sea that made my hair blow back.

And gradually my confused impressions merged into understanding.

The *Ardent* was my playground. I played on it not with other girls, or soft dolls, but with all the heavy, hard equipment of a man of war, and with any rough sailor that would pause in his sweating and striving to give me the time of day.

When we left the *Ardent* I was three years old.

The *Victory* was bigger. But soon I came to know it. For me it was a happy ship. The man with the stars on his coat who was its captain, often walked on the deck where I played in the quiet times. Sometimes he stopped when he saw me, and touched my head. Once he kneeled down and told me gently about his own daughter. His eyes were a quiet blue. And I loved the man whose words were calmer than the calmest sea.

What I remember most of all is the day he died.

A man at the topmast head shouted out: 'A sail on the starboard bow!' And everyone ran to the side.

Minutes later the blue ocean grew a forest of masts, sail-clouds billowing between them. At once the blue-jackets cheered and started stripping to the waist, and binding handkerchiefs round their heads to deaden the thunderstorm that was moving towards us in those looming clouds.

As we reached the enemy's line I was sent below as usual, where I lay listening to the dreadful sounds that came shattering from above – the splintering of wood and the cries torn out of men. Yet never a shot did I hear from our own ship till what seemed like a long time had passed. And I wondered what my father could be doing.

Then, when I thought we were going to be blown out of the sea, I heard the first orders to fire; and I felt for the first time how strange it was to be in the belly of a sea-going monster that spat murderous iron into flesh and blood, blew brains to smithereens, and shivered ships into swift surrender.

Soon the smell of powder drifted downwards to the cockpit where I lay in a little corner in a coil of hemp.

I heard the familiar shouts.

'Two points abaft the beam!'

'Point-blank now, point-blank! Fire, damn you!'

'You there, close up! Up with you, now!'

And before long the passageways were littered with panting sailors, their eyes rolling white and their mouths bubbling blood that glimmered among the dim lanterns. My mother walked about the shambles, carrying out of it what was worth saving. She and the surgeon were immersed in their trade, and the poor creatures they were helping hugged their wounds as if they were the only belongings they had left in the world.

So it was that no one noticed at first the man who was brought down the quarter-deck ladders by three seamen. But as he passed me where I lay, the handkerchief that was covering his face and chest slipped away, and I saw the stars, and looked into the face of the kindly man with the eyes like the sea. His face was pale. But when he saw me his tight lips smiled a little smile that I have never forgotten.

I bent down from where I lay to pick up the handkerchief. As I did so the surgeon ran over.

'Mr Beatty', said the man with the stars, 'this is no place for a child'.

'It is the place of carnage indeed', the surgeon said. 'But it is the safest place for her to be. And her mother is here.'

Then he said: 'But it is no place for your lordship either, and I hope you will not be down here long'.

'Alas, Mr Beatty', said Nelson, 'you can do nothing for me. My back is shot through. I have but a short time to live.'

Then they carried him, whispering, to another part of the cockpit, and laid him out on some spare sails. My mother was called from her work among the wounded to help the doctor to see to the worst wound of all that day.

They were there with him for a long time.

Once Captain Hardy came down and talked quietly to him. Then he went back up on deck.

Sometimes there were cheers from the gun decks above, and

when we were told that another of the enemy ships had surrendered, the man smiled up from his dark bed of pain.

I heard him call out a lot, asking for lemonade and wine and water. Over and over he said that he had done his duty, and he thanked God.

Once I went over to where he lay, and looked down at him.

He said: 'My daughter'.

Then I was hurried away by my mother.

Captain Hardy came back and whispered something to him. I saw Hardy kiss him, which I had never seen before between men. Then he kissed him again and left him.

When I looked at him again he was on his side. For a long time he was still, and I noticed that he had not finished his lemonade.

I never saw him move again.

A little later the ship suddenly burst into a sweet flowering of cheers, as we heard that our enemies were defeated. But the cheers withered almost as suddenly as they grew. Everyone was thinking about the great sailor, stretched out on his bed of sails.

Later my mother told me that she had dressed the corpse and embalmed it for burial in England. Lord Nelson had asked not to be thrown overboard.

I never saw any of that. But I saw a lot more that I can recall unaided, and much else besides that my parents reminded me of, kindling my recollection. I don't need reminding though, about Trafalgar. But for all the horrors I saw, what I'll remember most of all is standing deep below the ocean in the cockpit of the *Victory*. Young though I was, I was stilled by the sight of that one dead man. The life had ebbed from the body of the world's greatest seaman, and no force on earth could bring that tide in again. That made me cry.

Nowadays I think, what more fitting than a bed of sails to die on, for the sailor who had stood beneath their billowing clouds throughout so many great campaigns.

Old Rob was now part of the darkened room, in which the fire glowed dimly, like a ruby.

He told me the last of the story.

After the Battle of Trafalgar the seafaring trio stayed in service for another six months. Then the Watsons retired. They'd had enough of action and adventure for a lifetime, and with his bounties and prize-money Thomas wanted to do what he could to give his daughter a proper life on land. Mary too wanted a quiet life.

They returned to Cellardyke, and there they opened an ale-and-pie shop at the harbour head, hard by the scenes of Thomas's boyhood. In time, little Margaret had several brothers and sisters, though the Cellardyke folk were amused by the way she would always walk down to the pier to have a crack with the old seamen.

Eventually Margaret married a cooper and became Mrs Camble. She had a large family herself, but she outlived every single one of them, and lived on to tell this tale a thousand times.

'She's lying up there now in Kilrenny kirkyard', said Rob. 'You'll have seen the gravestone.'

It was not a question.

'Yes', I said. 'I've seen it many times. And her father's and mother's.'

Nor was that an answer.

It was after I'd gone home from school the next day that I learned that Rob had dropped like a stone while making his morning porridge. The funeral was at two o'clock on the Friday afternoon. I couldn't attend it. I was sitting my Higher History. It had loomed large into my life these past few weeks, but I sat it as if it had been an arithmetic exam, the large-sounding questions paling into insignificance the more I thought about them. The pros and cons of historical assessments, population figures, political reform, decisive battles – even the titanic personalities of the nineteenth century – they seemed to me as I wrote to be just the fringe of history, the debris washed up by the tide; to be combed through by future ages with no conceivable influence on the sea that sounded forever on their shores.

As I came out of the examination hall that afternoon, and walked past the turning barley towards Kilrenny, I thought that history in the long run is made up of people, and by people – but little people, like the Watsons; not the Napoleons and the Nelsons. The French marvelled at the superiority of the British naval gunnery, when their own ships and guns were technically better. Some would say it took men like Nelson to turn them into magic. Anyone who'd listened to Old Rob could more easily believe that gunners like Thomas Watson and women like his wife were what made the difference.

What did it matter for them now?

I walked over to Rob's newly made grave on which the scarred squares of turf had been stitched back together, over the wounded earth. In time there would be a headstone here.

I went across to the two headstones that I knew by heart.

ERECTED

BY MARGARET WATSON

IN MEMORY OF HER HUSBAND

JOHN CAMBLE 1801-1859

ALSO

MARGARET CAMBLE 1801-1892

THREE OF THEIR CHILDREN

LIE EAST OF THIS STONE

Beneath this simple stone lay the baby of the sea-battle – now a bundle of bones.

I stood for a while in front of the older stone.

ERECTED

BY MARY BUEK

IN MEMORY OF HER HUSBAND

THOMAS WATSON, MARINER

CELLARDYKE

DIED 17th DEC 1831 AGED 66

ALSO OF HIS WIFE

MARY BUEK WHO

DIED 28th FEB 1854 AGED 77

Walking round to the reverse side I read once again the simple epitaph.

> 'What though we wade in wealth or soar in fame,
> Earth's highest station ends in Here he lies.'

I sat down on the grass and leaned my back against the stone. I had with me a copy of Keith Feiling's *A History of England*. I was ironically struck by one of his sentences. Thumbing through the pages, I came to it. 'Few places are better known in England than the cockpit of the *Victory*.'

How many people in England knew about this simple Scottish headstone against which I had placed my back? Fewer places, I thought, could be more obscure. There wasn't even a record on it, however brief, of the things the Watsons had done, the places they had been. Like millions of others they had been too busy living and dying to worry about making history. People would pass this way among the insects that buzzed here on summer afternoons like this. They would stand in the long grasses that waved among these stones, and never know the violence that these simple sleepers had known; never dream the greatness they had touched, and which had touched them. A man could stand here within sight of the shimmering firth beyond, and never guess how intimate was the connection between the silent dust and that shimmering sea: Thomas Watson, Mariner. Nor could they think that those who lay in the cool and comfort of this sun-steeped old kirkyard had once tossed below the decks of a much darker world, even more crowded, even more confined.

I closed my eyes and turned my face to the sun.

Wine is a Mocker

I

THAT NEW YEAR, it was said by his congregation that the Reverend Ross Kinnear, of St Monans parish church, had drunk himself to death.

The backbiters in the flock nibbled busily during the nine days wonder that followed. But they could never really get their teeth into it, for there were certain facts that were indisputable.

For one thing Kinnear was as old as the hills when he died, and his anything but brief candle was long overdue the snuffing when it finally went out that winter.

For another thing the drink wasn't his only vice. He smoked like an unswept lum – even in the vestry, which stank of his cheap little cigars – and at weddings and funerals he stuffed his fat face like an ox. So that coronaries or cancers, or death in a dozen different disguises could have carried him off as easily as you like.

But Lizzie Reekie, the beadle's wife, who did the cleaning for both Dr Murray and the manse, swore that she heard him say to his assistant that alcoholic poisoning was what was down on the death certificate. And Dr Murray had said that he wasn't at all surprised. For the cellars of that manse were like a French chateau. The abomination was everywhere, in crates and cradles – wines, whiskies, rums – you name it, Kinnear had it. In the line of drink there had been nothing new under the sun as far as that man was concerned.

When he was finally transported to that cocktail cabinet in the sky, as Lizzie insisted that Dr Murray had said, the kirk elders were fairly itching to get their hands on all that devil's brew. The Women's Temperance Association planned to pour every last bottle of it into the harbour during an open air meeting. Following Kinnear's death that would be a powerful demonstration that God is not mocked, least of all by wine.

The trouble was that old Kinnear had no surviving family. Unlike him, all his relatives had had the decency to die long since. In the absence of a will, his solicitor, Mr Armstrong, who was also session clerk, insisted that there could be no question of their taking the law into their own hands.

'Even a dead man's drink isn't something that can be plundered at our pleasure', he said at the session meeting.

'Our best bet is to appoint a minister who shares our own distaste for the deadly stuff, and then to allow him, discreetly you understand, to dispose of it as he can.'

There was deflated agreement.

The Reverend Alastair McClintock had never been seen to take a drink in the twenty years of his ministry. Orange juice at weddings and ginger wine at Christmas – that was his strength. So his elders in Caithness wrote and said when their minister applied to come south.

Mr Armstrong, everybody was surprised and glad to hear, was in a position to confirm that. He had known Alastair McClintock when they were at the university together in Aberdeen, and unlike most students his tastes were decidedly not for beer. His application for the pulpit seemed to be the happiest of coincidences.

But the other applicant had the most exceptional qualifications. The Reverend Dr Henry Crawford had been educated at the Edinburgh Academy. He had graduated from Trinity College Cambridge before going on to New College to take his B.D. Then he had gone back to Cambridge to do his doctor's degree. His thesis was shortly to be published. All this, and he was only twenty-seven.

There were no other applicants but the session were well pleased with the field as it stood.

Old Mr Kinnear had died in his cups quite suddenly, and the third Sunday after his death was a communion Sunday. It was arranged that Dr Crawford would officiate during morning communion and that Mr McClintock would take the evening service. Those in the congregation who wanted to register a vote would have to attend both services – as they ought to be doing in any case. Otherwise their vote would be half blind.

From north and south each man was going to be travelling a fair distance, and Mr Armstrong suggested that they should both be put up at the empty manse. That would necessitate a meeting between the two, but after all they were civilised men of the cloth. Mrs Reekie said she would do an evening meal and bed and breakfast for two that weekend at the manse. For his part the session clerk took it upon himself to brief both men in the manse on the Saturday night. A minister wanted to know his kirk and community as surely as they wanted to judge him.

'Five star treatment, I'd say', said Mr Armstrong to the session. 'Barring the drink, of course', he added dryly.

And everybody laughed.

II

Lizzie didn't go in for fancy fare. There was nothing like kail and beef with mashed tatties and turnips to stick to your ribs on a bitter January afternoon.

After she had gone home, the two ministers sat on either side of a roaring fire in Kinnear's book-lined study, with Mr Armstrong in the middle.

The session clerk rose and walked over to a massive mahogany cabinet whose polished exterior mirrored the blaze from the hearth. He opened its dark double doors and a carved goddess halved herself to reveal a shimmering cluster of cut crystal decanters that winked and gleamed in the firelight. His fingers probed delicately among stoppered rubies and ambers.

'And now that the cat's away – a drop of brandy after dinner?'

'Oh, I don't see why not', said Dr Crawford. 'I've never been averse to a drink – and I see that Mr Kinnear wasn't old-fashioned enough to be afraid of the devil in the bottle.'

'Mercy me, Dr Crawford', said the lawyer, 'we'd better not let the session hear you speaking like that.'

The young man's face showed some alarm.

'But just between ourselves', the lawyer added, with a conspiratorial smile, 'I'm fond of a drink myself, and I don't at all share their bigotry.'

Dr Crawford looked somewhat relieved.

'Oh, they're a perverse and self-righteous generation up at that kirk', went on Mr Armstrong. 'The Scribes and Pharisees had nothing on them, let me tell you. One drop of sherry in your Christmas cake and the Temperance lot would have you damned to perdition with the most hardened of the local boozers.'

He poured Dr Crawford a generous golden glassful from the decanter.

'But', he said, tapping the side of his nose and winking hugely, 'we're men of the world, and what they don't know will never harm them. Now what about yourself, Mr McClintock?'

'By Jove', said the other minister, rising from his seat, 'this is something of a rarity for me, I may say. Do you mind if I have a little browse first?'

'Eh?'

'I mean among the decanters and things.'

'Oh my heavens, of course you can, Mr McClintock! You know, for one awful minute there I thought you were speaking about the blessed books.'

'God forbid I should be a spoilsport! No such thought in my head.'

He removed various stoppers, and after a minute or two of clinking and sniffing he returned to the fireside carrying a ship's decanter that was three-quarters full. He set it down on the nest of coffee tables by his chair. Mr Armstrong slipped out one of the tables and placed it between himself and Dr Crawford. Then he set the other decanter down on it and poured himself a glass. He raised it to one man, then to the other.

'Well, here's to both of you', he said, 'and to tomorrow. We can only keep one of you, mind, but I can see there's going to be no hard feelings when the day's over.'

Both ministers assured him that there was no question of that. They lifted their glasses to their lips and for a few moments the only sound in the flickering study was the crackling of the fire.

'My, that is a delicious brandy', said Dr Crawford. 'I've never tasted better.'

'Champagne cognac', pronounced the lawyer. 'Old Kinnear used to drink it like water. And there's a lot more stashed away in the cellar.'

He drained his glass, smacking his lips together.

'Still, mustn't be greedy. What's your poison, Mr McClintock?'

'Nothing so strong as your champagne cognac – but it's good stuff.'

'Well, I think I'll just have one more glass of this', – he poured himself a big one – 'and then I'll stick to the plonk.'

'If this is plonk then I don't know what heaven is.'

The session clerk lifted his elbow and emptied his glass for the second time. He breathed out a long, brandied sigh. Mr McClintock then leaned over and replenished his glass for him from the decanter at his side. Mr Armstrong did the same for the protesting Dr Crawford.

'Nothing but the best for a palate of discernment', he insisted.

For five minutes they drank without speaking, staring into the glowing coals.

At length Dr Crawford broke the silence.

'What are his books like anyway?'

'No idea', Mr Armstrong said. 'Have a look if you're really interested. Here take your drink with you.'

'Well, it's always useful to know what sort of mould your predecessor's mind's been cast in – Oh, I do beg your pardon, Mr McClintock, I really wasn't making any assumptions. I only meant if I were to become his successor. Slip of the tongue, I assure you.'

'Quite all right, I know what you meant.'

'Come and have a look yourself.'

'No thanks, I feel really at home here already. I'll just sit with my drink here and enjoy the fire.'

Glass in hand, Dr Crawford moved along the spine-covered walls, twisting his neck first to one side, then to the other, to squint at titles.

'Crikey!' he exclaimed. 'Will you look at this! Altizer's *The Death of God*. Mr Kinnear was into radical theology. Hans Kung: *Does God Exist?* – just published. I see Robinson there too, though even he's a bit dated now. And there's Richards: *The First Easter: What Really Happened?* He wasn't afraid of the liberal churchmen either.'

'Oh come and have another drink man. Don't talk shop.'

The session clerk stretched across and refilled the younger man's glass as he returned from the shelves, tripping over the carpet.

'Pretty amazing though', said Dr Crawford, wiping cognac from his shoe, 'for an old minister in a small place like this.'

'What's your own book about, Dr Crawford?' asked Mr McClintock.

'Oh, it's on the chronology of the Old Testament. That's what I did my thesis on.'

'The chronology of the Old Testament', murmured Mr Armstrong. 'Isn't the mere passage of time remarkable?'

Mr McClintock dipped his nose into his glass. Dr Crawford was still thinking about Mr Kinnear's library.

'A man's library', he said solemnly, 'is the index to his mind. Mr Kinnear's sermons must have been up to the mark.'

'Ah', said the lawyer, 'well I'm here to tell you that they weren't. They might have been at one time, but if you ask me it was the kirk here that finally drove Kinnear to drink.'

He gulped another glassful from Mr McClintock's decanter and proceeded to make business-like noises in his throat.

'I think it's about time I told you boys a thing or two about this kirk and community you're thinking of moving into. And the first thing I think you should both appreciate is that all this new-fangled stuff about God being depth, and resurrection just a state of mind, and hell a fairy tale and all that – that just won't wash outside these four walls. The Fifers like their religion straight. Hell and heaven just as they come, and not watered down. Talking of which, your glass is empty, Dr Crawford.'

The young minister's face was flushed.

'Do you seriously mean to tell me that a minister here, if he's going to survive, is going to have to throw away all the theological enlightenment of the last twenty years, and permit his congregation to, to. . . .'

'To live in the dark ages', said Mr McClintock.

Mr Armstrong looked at both of them.

'Well', he said, 'there was a man here tried to modernise things a bit. That was before Kinnear's time. But he didn't last long.'

'What happened?' Mr McClintock asked.

'They hung a walking stick on his door. Every Saturday night they used to do it, so that when the poor man came out to preach on the Sunday morning he'd find it there. You can just imagine how that would build up your confidence for the morning sermon. Eventually he took the hint and just walked off – straight off the end of the pier one night. He never even left a note.'

'But that's barbaric!'

'Ah, Dr Crawford, don't I know it! But there you are, you see. The Philistines are upon you.'

Dr Crawford filled his own glass this time. Mr Armstrong got up and flung two logs into the grate.

'Beechwood', he said. 'Kinnear's got a log-pile in his woodshed that would keep you burning till kingdom come.'

The fire that had embered down to a deep red glow came suddenly alive in a burst of flames. Against the black window panes there was a soft, thick flurry of snowflakes. Mr Armstrong rose again and closed the curtains.

'Oh', he said, coming back to his chair, 'I could tell you a thousand stories that would put these folk in their place for you.'

'I wish you would', Mr McClintock said. 'I dare say that there are certain similarities with my own parish up in Caithness. But

Dr Crawford here hasn't yet had the advantage of a church of his own, and there's a world of difference I'm sure between Edinburgh and Cambridge and this little neck of the woods.'

'That's damned generous of you.'

Dr Crawford's face glowed. 'Fire away, Mr Armstrong. The night's young, as they say, and so am I. Let me know what I'm in for.'

'On the condition', the session clerk said, 'that we all fortify ourselves with another drink.'

From the stopperless decanters three streams of gold flowed softly into three empty glasses that once more caught the firelight. And for a long time after that, the chime of crystal and the quiet ripple from decanter to glass were the only noises that broke the session clerk's monologue. Night had unlocked his tongue, and it ran loose.

Outside snow fell on snow.

III

Superstition. That's the first thing you've got to bear in mind. It's bred in their blood. It goes back centuries and it operates in more ways than you can get used to in a lifetime.

There's one thing you can be sure of, though. This is an old fishing community, and here the man in black has always been looked on as public enemy number one. However much they may put on a kirk face, these fisher folk, they'll be pursing their lips and fingering their beards at you the minute your dog collar is turned the other way. They'll come and listen to you on a Sunday, sure enough, as regular as you sound the bell, but don't you set your shoe in their territory, because I can tell you, you'll not be welcome. As sure as death they'd see a knot in your laces, or if you were whistling the hundredth psalm under your breath you'd be raising storms at sea like some old witch. Even the sight of you is enough to sour their faces. In the old days if they as much as met you on their way to the harbour they'd not take the boat out. And if you asked them if they were going to sea they'd as soon cut out your tongue as give you an answer.

It's not as bad as it used to be, but even today there's some old skippers won't even give you a handle to your jug. To them you're the man with the black coat, or the queer fellow, or white-throat – something like that. They used to call the kirk the bell-house.

They wouldn't mention salt or salmon either. Not so long ago there was a boat ran out of salt while they were at sea, and they hailed an English drifter. 'We want something we dinna want tae spik aboot!' was what they shouted. 'Is it salt ye want?' the Englishmen shouted back. And the whole crew dived below decks to drown out the echo of that awful word. Nowadays they call salmon redfish. You just say otherwise, you try to reason with them, or tell them that a rose by any other name would smell as sweet, and I can tell you, your own name would be pure mud.

I'll give you an example of a new minister who either through ignorance or education took no account of this kind of superstition. And this happened right here in St Monans in the very kirk that you're applying for.

On his first Sunday everybody crowded in to hear the new man, so that in the galleries upstairs they were packed like kippers.

No doubt the poor soul thought he was safe to preach on the parable of the Prodigal Son, maybe putting the old wine into a new bottle for fine effect. Well, he never even got the length of his sermon. When he announced that he'd be reading in Luke chapter fifteen at the eleventh verse, there was a dark ripple of tongues went through the kirk.

Maybe he thought it was one of their favourites. Anyway, he carried on reading in a hush like death, till he came to verse fifteen, where it says that the prodigal went to work for a man who sent him into his fields to feed the swine. He'd no sooner reached the last word in the verse when everybody hissed under their breaths, 'Touch cauld iron! touch cauld iron!' And they were all fiddling frantically in their pockets and looking about in desperation for something to touch.

Whether he carried on through stubbornness or stupidity, I don't know – but he was sorely misguided. He just got to the middle of verse sixteen, where it mentions swine again. It was too much for the congregation. Roaring like bulls to drown out the dreaded word before it poisoned their ears, they broke like a wave and surged out of the kirk. The folk upstairs dreeped down from the galleries onto the heads of them beneath. Some of them even jumped in their panic to get out.

There it was, you see. A kirkful of fishermen and all of them going to sea on the Monday. How else could they be expected to behave? At any rate, very few folk of the nether town came back to the kirk for many a Sunday to come, and as for that particular ministry, it was over without the first sermon ever being preached.

That story's going back a bit. But it shows you just how deeply superstitions like that had bitten into their lives. The fishers of today are descended from these folk. Today's taboos may not be as strong as yesterday's but the superstition is the principal thing.

Now that's how they want their religion, which to most of them is just an extension of their superstition. Just you try rationalising Christianity for them. You'll find yourself going down like a dish of cold kail.

Take miracles, for example. We hear nowadays that the miracle of the five loaves and two fishes consisted in Christ's influence on folks' better nature. He got them to bring out their sandwiches and their packets of crisps from where they'd stashed them, and pass them around a bit. By God, I can just see how that one would go down! No, they want a good old-fashioned miracle – a clear-cut line between the rational and the divine, between God and man, those outside the kirk and the ones inside, the boozers in the Cabin Bar and the members of the Temperance Association. Anything less than that and they'll hound you from the pulpit. It's bred in their bones you see, and fire won't burn it out.

Take that story I told you just now. That fear and hatred of pigs that it brings out for you once extended to the farmers who kept them, and the feeling is still kept alive in a less than neighbourly attitude to this very day.

In the old days it was really bad.

The town was divided, as it still is, by the brae, which has a fair steepness to it. The fishers lived down on the shore, naturally, where they could spread their nets on the links to dry. That was the nether town. Up at the top of the brae were the farmers who reared the very beasts the fishers believed to be cursed in scripture.

That arrangement was bearable, so long as the twain didn't meet. But you can see the weakness in the situation. The pigs were forever running loose. Just like the ones in the parable of the madman, they came careering down the brae towards the harbour. Any fisherman who set eyes on one had to let a tide ebb and flow before he would dare put to sea. That meant a lot of time and money wasted, because they took the superstition so seriously, you understand. And in those days people were really poor, so that there were times when their living became seriously threatened.

One night, after two wasted days on shore, the fishermen got together and voted to march up to the fields next morning, to teach the farmers a lesson in pest control. When the morning came they went up armed with boat hooks and grappling irons and Lord knows what. The farmers were waiting for them though, with scythes and pitchforks. God! Talk about beating your swords into ploughshares and your spears into pruning hooks. With that lot it was the other way about!

Now that could have turned out to be the bloodiest battle in the annals of the place, had it really opened out. As it happened, one of the farmers had the notion of bringing out the pigs as reinforcements, and they opened every gate of every hovel and shooed the beasts in the direction of the enemy. It was a military masterstroke. The pigs charged for the brae just as the fishers came to the head of it. They broke ranks and ran for their cottages with the pigs squealing and grunting at their heels and the farmers laughing themselves fit to burst.

Mind you, after that things couldn't go on as they were, and the Laird of Newark, having failed to convince the fishers that pigs were harmless enough creatures, was forced to decree their extermination or exile. You couldn't find a pig within a mile of St Monans for a hundred years or more afterwards. And the farmers didn't like that, you can be sure.

Things are not quite as bad as that today. Even so, you're not likely to find yourself marrying a fisher girl to a farmer too often. They still think of one another as foreigners.

Of course, the parable of the Good Samaritan is supposed to make you think the other way, isn't it? The Samaritans were the Jews' worst enemies, yet this one in the story was the only man who turned out to be a good neighbour to the Jew. Well, that's fine, for Jews and Samaritans, so long as you don't start trying to apply scripture to Shore Street and Cow Park Lane. Here among the fishermen the word 'ploughman' is still used as a term of abuse. So there's your congregation.

Divisions in the congregation. Well, that's something every minister has to put up with, you might say. But in most communities the world outside the kirk pays little heed to what goes on inside it. You won't find the same indifference here, I'm sorry to tell you. On the contrary, the place is a boiling cauldron of holy rivalries.

Picture yourself sitting down to tea, or maybe in the middle of writing the Sunday sermon. The door bell rings. You answer it, and a man in a raincoat, very neatly collared and tied and bowler hatted, asks you if you are saved. While you're still standing there, open-mouthed at the question, he is already shutting the gate, and you realise that he has put a tract into your hands. It may tell you, among other things, that there is no scriptural authority for salaried ministers. Mind you, as far as I'm aware, the bible doesn't expressly forbid a man to accept money for preaching the gospel: there is no scriptual authority against it either. But the man who has just left your door prefers the negative to the positive side of things. He is a member of the Brethern.

Picture yourself again on a quiet Sunday afternoon, the morning service over, your dinner just starting to digest. You switch on the radio, or pick up a book. Before you know where you are, your peace is shattered by an ear-splitting yell: 'Repent! Repent! Repent ye, for the kingdom of God is at hand!' You look out of your window, half expecting to see a long-haired maniac wearing goat-skins or something. But there instead is a gathering of people who look anything but demented. The Brethern are out there in force, all in their fawn raincoats and their leather gloves. And the one in the middle is shouting himself hoarse about damnation, and his right arm is raised, and his finger is pointing, it seems to you, ever so suspiciously in the direction of your own house. Let the guilty tremble – if the cap fits.

They take their stand everywhere, you see. For the devil has to be fought on the beaches and in the streets, as it were.

It wouldn't be so bad if there were just the one lot – it would take them all year to visit all the sinners in turn, you included. The trouble is, there's all sorts of them, Open and Close, and various little pockets and cells of theological and ecclesiastical resistance that have bees in their bonnets about some chapter and verse or other.

Some Sundays you've got three or four gangs of them positioned at strategic points all about the town, from the pub to the pier-head. Once they start volleying, all hell breaks loose, quite literally, and in between consigning all and sundry to the lake of the fire, they're excommunicating each other into the bargain. Sundays can be quite noisy. And if they happen to be holding an open-air meeting at the same time as the kirk is in – well, nobody's going to listen to a damned word you say for listening to them breathing fire outside. Not that they ever stand right outside the kirk, mind you, but believe me, these boys can shout.

I'll tell you one of the upshots of their carry on.

There's some families here are so literally divided in two, you wouldn't believe it. Don't ask me what the bible says about dining with sinners. All I know is that Christ was quite happy to sit down and take a bite to eat with them, and a drop to drink, for that matter. Anyway, there are some Brethern families where sons or daughters, or sisters or brothers break away from the group when they get older. When that happens their relatives won't eat with them. Even their own fathers and mothers won't sit down to table in the same room. And if you say anything to them about it, they'll tell you which bit of the bible justifies what they're doing. It's no good appealing to family love. Christ, they say, came to divide fathers from sons and brothers from sisters, and whoever followed Him would be his father and his mother, and so on. What about for the sake of peace then? Ah, but Christ came not to bring peace on earth, but a sword. That's what he actually said, Matthew Chapter 10 Verse 34. That's the trouble, you see, you can never outquote them.

When Kinnear pointed out to the head of one of these divided families that Christ sat in the same room as publicans and sinners, and took meat with them, this man – he was a joiner – rigged up a sliding wooden partition that cut the dining-room right in half. Right across the table too, it went, hatch and all, so that he and his sinning offspring were in the same room, but not actually eating together. So he satisfied the requirements of both St Matthew and St Paul at the same time. That was some happy medium, but at least it was a compromise. It sounds fantastic, but it's true. I can show you the house. You can even see the partition, if it's tea-time.

I went to one of their Gospel Hall services once, when I was younger. There's no music – no organ anyway, just the sound of droning voices. They'll tell you that music is an abomination. Salome danced before Herod and it cost John the Baptist his head. But what about David? He danced before God with all his might, and tells you in the psalms to praise God with music. That sounds good, out of context, but in reality David was just an old sinner, an awful man for the women. He couldn't keep his hands off other men's wives. It's quite clear from the bible, in fact, that God was none too pleased with David, so you needn't set him up as an example.

There's no telling who's going to preach either. They just sit there in silence. Then one of them gets up and starts to spout. He could go on for an hour, without notes. It's the spirit that's moving them, you see. Well, maybe it is, for you can look for the scrap of paper hidden in the bible, or the headings written out on the shirt-cuffs, but you won't find anything like that sort of trickery. They can talk, and no mistake. That's what makes them so formidable. And no one's questioning their sincerity.

Why not join forces with them then – iron out the differences?

Well, this ecumenical movement may be a great thing nowadays, but it falls on stony ground here. They don't want to know. I can just see the faces of the kirk session when you bring up the motion of a joint meeting with the Brethern! Or suppose you gently hint to the congregation that maybe there are some aspects of the Roman church thet they could benefit from. I can tell you what sort of a reaction you'd get.

I've been session clerk for donkeys years and lately the job's grown sour on me – you can see why. I'm a broad-minded sort of man, as you can appreciate, but for the rest of them, you might as well go and preach to the fish, like St Anthony, or whoever it was. They're the most bigoted creations on God's earth. Yet there's some of them are just whited sepulchres, and what's worse, they're known to be. In fact some of them are famous for it.

Take the Postie, for example. I don't mean the man that carries your letters. Rab Aitken is the man I mean – the Postie's just his nickname. He'll likely be session clerk after I retire, and he's as bent as they come. I'll not beat about the bush. To put it plainly, he's a bloody pervert. If knicker-knocking were his dead strength it would be sufferable, I suppose. But that's not as far as it goes with him. The fact is, he exposes himself – can you imagine? Well, it's a common enough weakness in some men, you may say, even if it's a bit much in an elder of the kirk. But with him it's worse than that. It's the way he does it – through letter boxes. He hasn't even the decency to do it in a park or standing at a window like everybody else. No, he's got to make a thing of it by posting his private parts through women's doors. That's why they call him the Postie.

There's a famous story I could tell you here.

There was this female worthy called Rona. She's dead and gone now, God bless her. She had a house at the east end of Shore Street, the very last house in the town it was, facing the sea. Anyway, every morning she'd greet the sun wearing just her knickers, nothing else. If you were down on the rocks you could see her doing her morning dance in front of her door. She was touched, poor soul, and the only ones who went to watch were a few bairns on their way to the baker's for the morning rolls.

Well, Rab couldn't keep away from Rona's door, and every so often he was tempted to advertise his presence in his usual way. He must have felt bashful about it though, because he always ran for his life immediately after the offence.

Now Rona couldn't imagine who this was, but she had knowledge enough of the world to recognise that it was a man. So she got to phoning nearly every dignitary in the town, sometimes in the middle of the night too, to ask them if they had been the postman that day. The headmaster, the provost, the policeman – even old Kinnear got a call. They were all outraged.

Eventually Rona decided to find out. She kept the fire tongs ready at the back of the door.

In the course of time Rab committed his next offence. She ran to the letter box and seized him fair and square, and she held on hard till he screamed for mercy and gave his name. The phone calls stopped after that, though at what cost to the Postie I don't suppose we'll ever know.

And yet this same man, with the second mark of Cain on him, will be the first to carp and complain if your sermons don't come up to his expectations of what is lovely and pure and proper, and of good report and all that.

Then you've got choice specimens like Geordie Jack, the leader of the choir. Proper mean he is, and a right jealous individual. He fairly sets at naught the biblical injunction that we should rejoice with them that do rejoice and weep with them that do weep. It's quite the other way about with him. He rejoices to see folk weep and weeps to see them happy. And yet he'll stand at the head of that choir and lead them like a musical Moses. He's got a voice like the last trumpet and a mouth to match. The only advantage of that huge gob is when he's singing. He opens it so wide you can't see his face, and that, believe me, is a blessing. They say he's worn the same suit to the kirk for the past forty years. That's his meanness for you. The jacket is so shiny you could shave in it. And there's some would say that's exactly what he does.

But there you are, you see, I'm beginning to sound like one of the blabbermouths.

Gossip – that's the other great sin around here. They sit down at the front of the harbour, these old bodies, with their caps pulled down over their eyes, just watching and listening, all day long. Just like old barnacles waiting for a bit of dirt to float by, to feed on. They'll chew on nothing at all, and it'll keep them going all day. Who? when? why? how long? They'll worry a question to a split hair with their whispers and still keep on paring away for all they're worth. They'll tell you the name of the bairn before the woman herself even notices she's pregnant. They'll tell you the sins of your great-grandmother and visit them on your children yet unborn. Oh, they're great weavers of tales are our gossipers. The town tapestry's not complete without them. Their tongues go in and out like a shuttle on a loom. And that's the way it will be with them until death shuts them up.

IV

The three men were staring into the dead wreckage of the fire. The decanters stood unstoppered and empty like broken monuments from an age ago. Dr Crawford wore a white blind sort of look on his face. The other two men seemed a little drawn and pale.

The session clerk rose and parted the curtains. A whiteness like death entered the room. The village was shawled in snow that seemed to hide every trace of the character he had given it the night before.

'Fancy that', he said. 'It's morning already.'

'Pleasure and action make the hours seem short', said Mr McClintock.

Dr Crawford blinked hard. 'Good Lord, that's very impressive, very impressive. I couldn't quote like that at this time in the morning. Eh? Did you say morning? Is it really morning?'

'Morning it is.'

The session clerk yawned and stretched.

'We've caroused till the second cock, I'd say, if it's quoting you're on for. And before the bird crows a third time you'll be giving us all a quote or two of your own, no doubt. For all that you say you can't?'

'Oh God! I feel terrible. Do you two feel as bad as I do?'

Mr McClintock shook himself.

'I don't know how any other man feels, but I'm ready this morning to give them all I've got – right from the shoulder. I take it that was the object of the briefing, Mr Armstrong?'

The session clerk brightened.

'I'm right glad that's the way you've taken it, Mr McClintock. It was a case of make you or break you. But my mission is only accomplished if Dr Crawford here feels the same way about it. Dr Crawford?'

I'm with you all the way. If we present a united front then they've no choice but to go forward. To bow down to the ways you've described would be unthinkable.'

He tried to stand up but he clapped a shaky hand to his head and sat down again.

'Right!' said Mr Armstrong, looking pleased with things. 'Then let's clean this place up a bit, and ourselves – I see you're feeling a wee bit groggy, Dr Crawford – Mrs Reekie will be here in a while to give you men your breakfast. I'd better make myself scarce.'

V

The Reverend Doctor Crawford ascended the pulpit like a ghost.

But he had no sooner opened his mouth than everybody could see that he was an angry ghost. His choice of reading was right enough: St John Chapter 2 Verses 1-11, Christ's first miracle in Cana of Galilee, where he turned water to wine at the wedding where they'd run dry. A fine choice for a communion Sunday. No doubt he'd be telling them how that miracle was like the miracle of the communion which they were all about to take. You could see that coming a mile away. But that was all right – you wanted nothing too complicated, nothing that would make you concentrate so hard on your pan drop that you'd bite it in two. No, you wanted what was obviously coming – a nice, clear, traditional message that you could suck in tune to.

Everybody was rightly shocked when the man in the pulpit started to tell them that what happened in Cana was no miracle, in the usual sense of the word. Christ wasn't a cheap sensationalist, on a level with a stage magician who did tricks for the bairns. Some folk still saw him like that, no doubt, and if Christ were walking this earth today, they'd be the kind who'd be wanting him to do his own variety show on the box. But people who thought like that were not true Christians. Hadn't Christ turned his face against miracle mongering when he refused the devil's request to turn stones into bread? Not that there would have been anything wrong with it if he had turned water into wine. For Christ was no killjoy, no Holy Willie. He liked a drink, and why not? To despise the material things of this world is a wrong-headed attitude in a Christian. For God made the world and He saw that it was good. But the real point about John Chapter 2 was that anyone who truly knew Christ found his water turned to wine every day of his life. For him the ordinary became wonderful, ordinary everyday living turned into a perpetual wedding, a wedding of the human and the divine, celebrated in the wine of the communion.

After that he went right off the rails altogether. He started to talk about all sorts of weddings – wedding yourself to other churches, and to your neighbour, and dissolving all rancours and differences in that great common cup.

It was obvious the man was raving. Anyone could see that from what he was saying – or trying to say, because he kept stumbling over his words and stuttering and slurring so badly you wondered if nerves had made him ill.

Soon it became clear to the whole kirk that Dr Crawford was in fact far from well. He had looked a sickly enough specimen when he first stepped up to speak. But now, in the middle of a sentence, he suddenly went whiter than the snow outside. He seemed to choke on something. Then he quickly stepped down from the pulpit and whispered something to the church officer, who ushered him away in the direction of the vestry. They were speedily followed by the session clerk.

During the electrified minutes that followed, the whisper went round starting from Lizzie Reekie's pew.

'He's as fou 's a puggie!'

Lizzie had served breakfast at the manse that morning and as God was her witness she had smelt drink in the air. Furthermore Dr Crawford had slipped and fallen in the snow coming into the kirk. Geordie Jack had laughed at this but Rab Aitken had said that he'd probably been throwing old Kinnear's cognacs down his neck the night before. The exhibition he had just put on seemed to leave the matter in no doubt. There was tremendous excitement. What a scandal!

Then, calm as you like, Mr McClintock appeared from the back door, behind Mr Armstrong and Mr Reekie. In a quietness you could cut he stepped nicely up to the pulpit and faced the congregation with a kind of sad reverence.

As Dr Crawford was indisposed, he said, he would take the remainder of the service himself. He did express the hope that Dr Crawford's unfortunate illness would not be held to militate against him. However, as he could see from the pulpit bible what the text for the day had been, he would say a few words of his own on that head, unprepared as he was.

VI

That Jesus turned water into wine, let there be no doubt about it.

But we ought to pay some attention to precisely what kind of wine it was that Jesus miraculously produced.

What does the master of ceremonies at the wedding actually say to Jesus? He says this: 'Every man at the beginning doth set forth good wine; and when men have well drunk, then that which is worse: but thou hast kept the good wine until now'.

The wine that Jesus produced is specifically pointed out to be 'the good wine', as opposed to the inferior variety they had been drinking before He came on the scene.

Now that word 'good' is as accurate a pointer as a label on a modern day bottle. For while we of today describe wine as good in proportion to its power to intoxicate, the people of Christ's day thought quite the reverse. Pliny, Plutarch and Horace all agree in describing the good wine as the harmless variety, *poculo vini innocentis*.

It is thus safe to presume that Christ deliberately created for the wedding party a much milder wine than they had been drinking: a non-alcoholic variety, in fact, the pure, unfermented juice of the grape, and not the potent poison that passes for good wine today.

But today there is among us an even more pernicious poison than wine. It is a breed of churchmen who would try to de-mythologise Christianity. Their interpretation of our text would no doubt be that it simply shows how Christ makes the mundane into something marvellous. Now that in itself is true, but it is only an additional truth. Anyone who makes that the central meaning of the passage is not only denying the miracle, but ignoring the point about temperance that Christ was implicitly making, and that the master of ceremonies makes explicitly when he describes His wine as 'good'.

And what man or woman who has read the scriptures can possibly afford to ignore Christ's lesson? 'Wine is a mocker, strong drink is raging: and whosoever is deceived thereby is not wise.' (Proverbs Chapter 20 Verse 1.) The truth of that is amply borne out by the bible, from Genesis to Revelation. Look what Lot did to his daughters when he was drunk. Look at that great whore of Babylon, drunk with the wine of her fornication.

But in the cup that we drink of today, let us partake of the true vine, and turn away from all others.

VII

The Women's Temperance Association were utterly ecstatic. And there wasn't a man or woman who didn't vote for Mr McClintock. He took the evening service as well, and there he said many heart-warming things. He was the hero of the day. By that time Dr Crawford was well on his way south.

It was late that night when Mr McClintock answered the door of the manse, where Mrs Reekie had served him a sumptuous meal. He was tired, but as he opened the door there was a glint in his eye.

'Mr Armstrong is it – or should I say David?'

'Aye, it's me Alastair – or should I say Mister McClintock?'

They chuckled their way through to the study, where a new fire was burning. The session clerk grinned wickedly, rubbing his hands.

'Well, Alastair, you'll be up north again tomorrow. But we'll be seeing you in a few weeks time. You were sensational', he added.

'And you last night – that was some display. How have you been since?'

'Oh, all right, but I've been peeing out iron brew all day!'

'Same here. I thought you'd let all the gas out of it. I've been dying for a drop of the real thing. Let's have a snifter now.'

Mr McClintock skipped to the cabinet and swung open one flank of the goddess. He brought out a decanter and filled two glasses.

'Good health.'

'Cheers. By the way Alastair, how *do* you propose to dispose of all the stuff in the cellar?'

Mr McClintock made his mouth into a whistling shape and narrowed his eyes.

'Dispose of it? Oh, let me see. I'd say fifty fifty would be fair, wouldn't you?'

'Oh aye. I'd say fifty fifty would suit me just fine!'

They drained their glasses.

And for several minutes the walls of the old manse echoed with hearty laughter, the like of which it had never heard, even in Mr Kinnear's enlightened days.

Exorcism

ELSPETH HAD never wanted to leave Glasgow in the first place.

She was a city girl, born and bred. The streams of traffic circulating the streets were the life-blood that glittered in her veins. She liked nothing better than to feel the beating heart of her habitat, to wander through its loud noons, its neon evenings. As she lay in bed, she enjoyed the distant hum of cars, the glow of lights in the night sky, and the feel of being wrapped in the comforting layers of a million other lives. She would no more have dreamed of living in the country than of inhabiting a graveyard.

So when Graham came home later than usual one evening to tell her that old Dr Hinchley, the chief criminal pathologist for the east of Scotland, had died, and that he had been recommended for the post, Elspeth thought that the world would stop spinning on its axis. Yet she knew this was a revolution she could scarcely deny. The new post both recognised and demanded the full stretch of her husband's abilities, and at nearly twice the salary. Added to this, Dr Hinchley had died leaving his large family house to be used as a tied dwelling, rent-free, to his successors.

Redwells, in the east of Fife, was one of these substantial eighteenth century country residences graced by its own grounds. Its rooms had blent as laboratory, office and home for the old man who had lived and worked there for nearly half a century. It was worlds from anywhere. The hamlet of Dunino, near St Andrews, was nearly two miles away, and the town itself was another ten – Elspeth gloomed at the thought. But Graham was spellbound by the prospect of being able to carry out much of his work from his own home, and so to see more of their three year old Katie.

It was the little girl's response that made Elspeth embrace the situation with a smile in the end. She danced like sunlight across the floor when she heard she was to have a garden. Their flat was high in the clouds, and from time to time even Elspeth had winced as she watched her wisp of apple-blossom fluttering strangely among concrete, steel and plaster – Rapunzel in a tower-block, laughter shut in by the bolts and shackles of convenience.

Even so, the hour of their departure was still-born for Elspeth.

The car sped silently along the miles of umbilical that reached back to Glasgow and yet were bearing her painfully away from it, out of the warm womb of her past and into an alien world. When at last the car delivered her to the doorsill of her future and its engine died away on the silence, she felt naked and raw, and ready to cry.

But Katie saved her, took her by the hand and clothed her with sunlight. As soon as the front door was open she was into passageways and up staircases in a trice, sprinkling rooms with the baptismal blessing of her welcome, dripping her silvery laughter through the house like a spring rain. She was the new spirit of the mansion, it seemed, bringing life between its tired old walls, unshuttering its dreary past.

'Mum! Mum! Dad! Quick, come and see!'

Following the harmless will-o'-the-wisp they came to the back of the house. Katie was dancing in front of the French windows, wide-eyed at what she saw – an antique stone pond and fountain, long waterless, but massively commanding the centre of the lawn. The correct key was produced and she streaked across the grass, scattering honey from the barley-field of her hair, sowing the garden with song. Soon she was orbiting the pond like a star gone mad, her hands clapping ecstatically. Her parents stepped out into the sunlight and followed her down the garden.

The ancient ornament was a magnificent white ruin. Twice the height of a human, the fountain was a lissom goddess. One arm bent downwards like a swan's neck to clasp a cherub to her milkless breast. The other was straight uplifted, bearing high above her classical contours a massive stone bowl, from the centre of which water must have spouted skywards, cascading past the brimming dish into the pond below. But how long since water-blossoms flourished here? The fountain was like a flower that had lost its fragrance.

Still, nature itself was attempting some work of compensation. Golden lichens had partly clothed the goddess's nakedness, stealing across her flanks and breasts, a modest caress effected over generations, a gentle touch of Midas. Mosses had strewn their glossy-green velvet cushions about the cracked bed. Dead leaves lay in the deepest parts that sloped down to the middle, and draped their changing tapestries across the outer rim. Now and then one or two detached themselves in the light breeze, little skeletons, and whispered the stories of their vanished lives against the dumb stone. Here was peace and beauty and a feeling of passion spent.

But there were other impressions too – of death's slow weather-
ings and time's decay. There was sterility and dryness where there
should be flowing patterns of light and sound.

'I want this working again', Elspeth said.

Graham had rather liked the battered beauty of the old stone-
work. But Elspeth was for movement and music, and Katie's voice
was loud for water over the next few days.

The man who came from the estate maintenance firm in Cupar
shook his beard at it, reckoning that the repair work to the mas-
onry would be costly enough in itself, plus the cost of buying and
fitting a large pump. Still, they could now afford the pretence of
living like lords and ladies. Three workmen arrived the following
morning.

They scooped out the surface vegetation and began lifting the
shattered stones from the weed-grown bed. Elspeth took Katie out
of their way, and went upstairs to mount a campaign on the attic.
Graham was downstairs in his professional apartments, still in the
toils of moving in. For some time Elspeth slaved among slanted
sunbeams, her lungs filtering the flecks of silvery dust. Her throat
had just begun to clamour for coffee when she heard one of the men
shouting her husband's name.

Clambering down the steep stairs with Katie in one arm, she saw
Graham following the man out of the French windows. She made
coffee and sandwiches and took them out on a tray. Katie followed
her with her glass of lemonade.

'What's so interesting then?' Elspeth asked, coming up with the
tray. All four men were bent like hoops over the pond. They stood
up as she spoke and she could plainly see how the dark brown earth
where the stones had been raised was streaked with white. So these
were the bone-bright roots of the great stone flower. Katie said it for
them between gulps of lemonade.

'Bodies!'

'Hardly, wee girl', said Graham. 'Just one skeleton.'

One of the workmen spluttered at father and daughter's matter-
of-factness.

'It's my work you see', Graham explained.

'Katie knows all about bones and things', added Elspeth.
'Graham, what does this mean?'

'It means', Graham said, gently detaching his arm, 'that the first
thing I've got to do is to phone the police.'

Four hours later a detective inspector and sergeant and two

constables watched impassively as Graham brushed away the last of the soil from the bones.

'Katie was right to use the plural', he said. 'There are two of them here, but not what we might have expected.'

Elspeth put a sudden hand to her mouth as she saw finally the truth that the fountain had concealed.

One skeleton lay prostrate in the soil, staring out at them from naked bones. The other made her turn away feeling heartsick and sad. It was pitifully tiny – that of an infant, half-rolled over onto its side towards the vanished rose of the other's breast. It had known neither crib nor coffin. The fleshless arm of the adult still retained the gesture of caress.

'Woman and child, sir?' asked the inspector.

'Yes, it's a woman, inspector. But I might as well tell you that you're scarcely needed here. From the look of the infant I would say it's highly likely that the mother died in childbed. The baby might have been stillborn or died soon afterwards – there's no telling. But one thing's sure.'

'What's that, sir?'

'If there was foul play of any kind, no one's ever going to be charged for it.'

'Why not, sir?'

'These bones could be hundreds of years old. Certainly as old as the fountain itself.'

Graham learned little more from his tests than he had already known, other than that the adult had been very young, and the baby a girl. The police moved off to fresher mysteries following his official confirmation that the bones were in the region of two centuries old. They were happy to leave him with whatever burial arrangements or historical researches he cared to pursue.

The minister of the parish church at Dunino proved helpful on both counts. He ushered them into his wide-windowed library, beaming at Katie as she flitted past.

'The Lumsdaines', he mused. 'Yes, they arrived here from the west of Fife in the late eighteenth century – family of builders, they were – and built Redwells. Of them there is little I can tell you, for the house passed out of their hands almost at once, and was bought by the ancestors of Dr Hinchley, who owned it until his death. The Hinchleys are all buried at St Andrews, actually. Henry Lumsdaine, who built the house – not an attractive character, I don't think –

he went abroad soon after his wife and child died. And that's about all I know, I'm afraid.'

'And where are they buried?' Graham asked.

'Why, right here in our own churchyard. Come and I'll show you.'

The silver-haired old gentleman led the way out of the manse and through his strawberry patch. Pausing to offer Katie a handful of tiny red moons, he took them through the gate in his garden wall that formed part of the churchyard boundary.

They followed him through a crazy clutter of urns and angels, pillars and tombs, commemorating in their changing fashions the dead of generations. Infants and octogenarians, burgesses and bricklayers, rose-lipped girls and sour-breasted spinsters lay frozen beneath the graveyard's green wave. They no longer sought the sun. The April rain-spears, piercing the earth's sides, would never quicken their silent dust. Elspeth shuddered at the scene, appalled by death's terrifying peacefulness, the awful finality of rest.

The minister stopped in front of one of the large table tombstones of the eighteenth century and waved a hand across it. Elspeth read the words slowly. The letters were inlaid with the ancient gold of lichen, a natural enrichment of what was otherwise a cold, formal record.

BENEATH THIS STONE

ARE DEPOSITED THE MORTAL REMAINS

OF CHRISTINA LUMSDAINE 1767-1792

AND OF HER DAUGHTER

CATHERINE LUMSDAINE 1789-1792

ERECTED BY HER SISTER ELIZABETH JANE GIFFORD

'So mother and daughter died together.'

Elspeth was thinking aloud. 'Just like the ones beneath the fountain.'

'Ah yes, unfortunate business', murmured the clergyman. 'Most peculiar into the bargain. Still, these were violent times, violent times, and they will receive a good Christian burial here just as if they'd died yesterday. In any case, their souls are long past bodily concerns.'

'Yes, but what about the Lumsdaines', Elspeth persisted. 'How did they die?'

'Er, I've no idea, my dear.'

The minister glanced at her quizzically through flashing spectacles.

'Does it matter how they met their end?'

Elspeth looked across to where Katie was gathering daisies. The grass was thickly starred with them, and the yellow suns of dandelions blazed between them, bright againt the green. Butterflies danced in silent ecstasy around the stones, and plunder-laden bees went booming past, dropping their golden bombs as they went.

'It's just a rather odd coincidence, both these small girls dying with their mothers, and both connected with that – with our house.'

'Oh, but in these days, my dear, infant mortality was high, terribly high. That's why they had such large families, you see. Why, in this churchyard alone there are scores of tiny skeletons lying beneath our feet, just as common as . . .'

Katie came up and presented him with a handful of scented white stars.

' . . . as daisies', he concluded with a smile.

That night Elspeth rose from a sleepless bed. She put on a dressing-gown and slippers, walked out into the garden and stood by the still fountain. What secret had been buried along with these bones? And what was the connection between them and those in Dunino churchyard? Had there been any mother and daughter in the house since those times? Surely. And yet, Dr Hinchley had lived a bachelor here for fifty years.

She glanced up and took in her breath sharply. She had never really seen the stars through the city's garish glow, and the sight chilled her to the bone, made her blood creep and her nerves tingle. So many! And all of them burning to waste, rusting there against the sky. They were scattered like seeds in the dark. Where was the hand of the sower among all this soundless withering? She shivered and went inside, quickly sought the oblivion of her pillow.

The work on the pond took nearly three weeks to complete.

On the last morning Graham had to attend a court hearing. Elspeth decided to have the water flowing for his afternoon return. The men switched on, and the stone burst into flowering song. Katie went wild with delight.

She demanded that the entire nursery of dolls be brought to

worship the great silver rose. She tottered across the lawn holding life-sized Mandy in a bear-hug. But Mandy's own little baby was missing. Elspeth remembered the doll had been left in the attic on the day the secret of the fountain had been exposed. She quickly ran upstairs. The doll was lying among a jumble of things against the far wall. She waded over to it, stumbled slightly, and put out a hand to steady herself.

At once she felt her finger-tips touching something that seemed warmer than plaster and softer than wood. She looked up. There was a small space between rafters and wall which her fingers had entered. Standing on tiptoes she peered into the gloom of the aperture. Neatly tucked away was what looked to be the edge of a slim book. She tried to pull it out but it was tightly wedged. She brought over a chair, reached in with both index fingers, and pulled hard.

Out it came – a plain, calfskin-bound volume, blotched with mildew and musty with age. Delicately she raised the front cover. The flyleaf was blank and badly foxed. She turned another page. There was a name at the top right corner, a name written in faded brown ink that she had seen spelt out in gold in Dunino churchyard. The name was Elizabeth Jane Gifford. She turned another leaf. There were the words *The Diary of Elizabeth Jane Gifford*. Unconsciously sinking into a sitting position, she turned the page gently and started to read.

It was to begin with a catalogue of mundane items, of some significance to the social historian perhaps, but devoid of immediate human interest. Elspeth was on the point of closing it when her eye caught a longer entry.

'23rd October 1791. This evening exceedingly wretched and miserable. Henry, God help us, has forced poor Jenny, and has gotten her with child. The poor girl, it seems, has been terrified out of her senses, and has only just confessed this to us. We are keeping her close in the house. She is five months from her time, and it is a wonder this awful affair has not been disclosed until now, for we knew nothing of it. My poor sister is wounded to the heart that his depravity has extended thus far. His debaucheries have been much to bear of late, but the shame of this latest act quite appals us. For Jenny, poor child, she only has fears for what her family will say, for she comes of good folk. God knows what is to become of the child of so shameful a union, or what outcry will succeed if this thing be discovered. Thank heaven our servants are gone! Little Cathy prattles on for her father, innocent of what a wretch he has come to be.'

So this was it.

But what was the sequel? Elspeth ceased to follow individual words and began to skim the entries at speed, to gather the drift of the sorry tale. The leaves spoke to her in gray whispers as they rose and fell through her fingers like the turning seasons. Eventually there broke the grim dawn of understanding.

'3rd March 1792. May I never live through such a night as this! An infant dead on its dead mother's breast, and the childbed the grave of both. Henry has been bereft of his reason for this long time past, and tonight he is gone quite crazed.

'The same night. Haunted by remorse, in a horrible state of drunkenness, and wholly lost to reason, he has buried his shame and guilt deep in the garden. He talks wildly of sealing the awful secret, to which we must be sworn, with a penitential monument. Alas, he is quite raving. It is the awfulest imaginable thing.'

The rest did not need imagining. It was unnecessary to read any further. Mechanically Elspeth turned to the last page of writing.

She froze.

'... and so the sweetest work of nature, our little Catherine, has perished in that accursed spot, drowned at her innocent play, and her mother, my most unhappy sister, followed her to the grave. And on the very day that water first flowed from it. Well might it gush forth from the ground the blood of the innocent that has now been stilled in the dearest of veins!'

Elspeth felt the coldness gather in her breast, the blackness in her blood. So Christina Lumsdaine had committed suicide, in all probability? But that was not what her brain was searching for. What drowning memory was struggling to break the surface of her consciousness, causing her almost to suffocate, to want to scream?

Katie.

'Oh, my God!'

She struggled to the skylight, her legs treading water, her stomach awash. How long had she been sitting here, lost in these withered leaves? Where was Katie? She looked down into the garden and gripped the edges of the open skylight hard at what she saw. Her mouth moved soundlessly, like someone under the sea. She saw what she had known she would see – a little wisp of apple blossom floating face downwards on the surface of the pond, drifting round on the shimmering sunlit shallows, the jets of water from the fountain playing over her like liquid gold.

For several seconds Elspeth gazed at the scene as if it were an illuminated page from that ancient diary, tragically, prettily unreal. Then the mask of her face melted into a running mixture of pain and horror and she turned and hurtled down the stairs. She reached the landing, skidded violently on the sanded floor and went crashing down the second flight. As she hit the passage wall at the base her skull exploded like a bursting star into a million miles of empty space, and as she floated through the bodiless regions at the speed of light she heard a familiar voice calling her name.

'Elspeth. Elspeth.'

The voice kept on calling her. It was Graham's voice, of course. But from where? And why? What was happening? She tried to sit up, the black universe inside her head burst into a galaxy of lights, and she turned weightlessly about. As she struggled to right herself she heard Graham's voice saying something.

'Let's leave sitting up till tomorrow, shall we? Concentrate on opening your eyes first. Can you do that?'

From within the dark sphere of her head Elspeth pulled up two sun-scorched blinds and instantly found herself looking out on the daylight world of her own bedroom. The universe contracted to its four flowery walls. Graham was standing at the foot of the bed.

'You're going to be fine, my lass, don't worry, it's just concussion mainly, though it's been pretty severe.'

'But Graham . . . you don't . . . Graham . . . how long have I been . . . Katie! Oh God, Katie!'

'I'm here, mum.'

The tinkling bell of her voice at Elspeth's side was followed by the sweet tickle of butterfly breath against her cheek. She reached out. A small hand encircled her forefinger like a band of gold.

'I came home to find Katie going frantic over you', said Graham.

'But Katie was in the pond! I saw her! She was. . . .'

Now, now, now, you're still concussed. Either that or you should have your eyes tested. Mandy was having a fine old swim in the pond, though. I got myself soaked doing a rescue operation there. Katie wants me to do a full post-mortem on her! Poor old Mandy. But we have to get poor old **mum better** first, don't we?'

'But Dad, Mandy is still full of water! Mum, tell silly Dad you're better. Mum, tell him to take the water out of Mandy now. Mum!'

But Elspeth was not listening to them any more. She was space-travelling again. And somewhere in her universe there formed the spirit of an exorcism.

Farewell and Adieu

LET ME tell you a simple, sad little story, that is connected with a
vast historical enterprise. It took place in Anstruther in the sixteenth century.

In 1588, after the defeat of the Spanish Armada, the surviving
vessels made their way up through the North Sea, round the north
of Scotland, through the Atlantic, and eventually reached Spain.
Thus much history acquaints us with.

What we also know to be true is that a Spanish vessel lay off
Anstruther for a time before continuing her way north, and her
crew was civilly received by the town's magistrates. There are
accounts of this in the session records of both Anstruther and Crail.
What the name of the vessel was, these records do not say, but my
account gives it as *Nuestra Señora de Cavadonga*.

At this same period there lived in Cellardyke a retired skipper
whose name was Learmonth. He had two sons, James and Andra,
and a daughter named Isobel. It is from the Learmonth family
papers – letters and other documents – now in the Public
Records Office of Scotland, that I have managed to piece together
this story.

Old Learmonth, it seems, was always first down to his boat in the
mornings. All the other Anster men would still be fast beneath the
waves of sleep, or rubbing eyes as dim as dawn. Meantime he'd be
stepping down the brae to push out the little yawl he still liked to
potter about in, carrying his sixty years as lightly as the summer
skies.

On that momentous morning, though he rose from his pallet at
four o'clock – an hour that was early even for him – he found his
lines ready-baited for him by the back door. Isobel was bending
over a new made fire, on which a pot of porridge was bubbling a
quiet song.

Isobel Learmonth's mother had died when she was seven, and for
twenty years she had filled her place, in looking after her father and
two brothers. Many's the young fisher lad had come to old William's
door, his heart pounding like the surge. Isobel, it has to be noted,

was a fair-haired charmer, as sweet as strawberries and morning milk. She grew in that rather dark house as naturally as a hawthorn blossom on a hedge, and not a fisherman around had ever succeeded in plucking her from her stay.

Often enough Learmonth's heart would grow quiet for sadness as he thought over his daughter's lot: rising in the dark dawns to the hearth's cold heart, making meat for her kin, baiting the lines, mending the nets – and all the while filling the house with a fragrance that should have smelled sweet in the nostrils of a man of her own.

But she would not be persuaded.

The fisher folk of her generation had married elsewhere, and now she was past the age when the younger ones would dream of asking her. The flower grew fuller on its stalk, and no one any longer thought to take it.

'You're up right early, lass', Learmonth said, sitting down to his dish of oats.

'Oh aye, it's the birds wakening me early these summer mornings', said the girl. 'Are James and Andra stirring yet?'

'Them? They're lying as low as leadweights and you'll not see them for an hour yet. My lines will be jumping with haddocks before they've tasted these oats.'

He rose from the rough table where the family faced each other between sleep and work in a sweet, salt circle.

'Mind you, they do a good day's fishing, these lads', he said. 'But they'll be staring the sun in the face by the time they're on their pins this morning. You go back to bed now, Isobel.'

'No father, I'll get them up and seen to. Down to the boat with you now. You like to be first out.'

'It's a man of your own you should be seeing to, my wee lass', Learmonth said.

He stood in the doorway a moment, his roughened old hand held gently on his daughter's head.

'Father, I'm not a wee lass, I'm twenty-seven years on this earth, and even if I wanted one, what man's going to take me now? Do you think they'll be putting in at the pier asking for my hand?'

Over the old man's left shoulder a splash of blood appeared between sea and sky, reddening the corn and honey of his daughter's hair. He kissed her on the crown of her head and smiled. But he sighed as he shouldered his basket of lines and swung down to the sea.

The yawl was lying on the lip of a full tide. It was lying alongside the larger vessel that the two brothers worked at this time of the year. Learmonth laid the lines in the middle of the boat's belly and shouldered the craft into the dark water.

Then he looked up for the first time.

The thick white whiskers about his lips suddenly parted. His eyes rounded. He sat there in the boat, staring, a silent statue on the dead flat calm.

Right inside the harbour it was – a huge hulk rising between himself and the open sea, a vessel of proportions his firth-bound eyes had never witnessed. Even the great Dutch herring busses seemed like skiffs in comparison with this.

As he sat and stared, the sun's rim broke the skyline, and poured a torrent of gold soundlessly into the sea. It flowed over the Forth and into the small harbour, and bathed the alien colossus in the first light of the morning.

The ex-skipper's eyes took in huge masts with furled sails, a web of riggings, silent flags, a row of gunports, and brasswork that gleamed and sparkled, responsive to the first fires of day that were now kindling the firth.

A voice cracked the golden stillness of the hour.

'Señor! Señor!'

In a bright flash Learmonth understood.

The Spaniards had landed at last. This was the unholy horror that the Reverend Mr James Melville had preached to them about, Sunday after Sunday, these past two months; and now, in spite of God, the true church, wind and weather, and the English navy too, here it was in all its insolence. Ready, no doubt, to blast and burn the village from pier to steeple in the name of popery.

'Señor! Señor!'

The old man did not wait to tangle with the foreign tongue. Before the caller had repeated his salutation, Learmonth was floundering for the shore. As he staggered up the steep brae he had come down so blithely, his yawl drifted quietly towards the harbour mouth and the flashing fire of the galleon that was anchored just inside.

Half roads up the slope he saw the figures of his sons descending. They stopped dead when they saw their father.

'Andra! Run up to Melville's manse as fast as you can, and tell him the Spaniards are here!'

The two men looked at each other and smiled.

'Then come and see', said Learmonth.

He went between his sons, and with an arm of each gripped hard in his own he hurtled them ten paces to the bend in the brae. Three stood there and stared, black etched against gold.

Then Andra was racing eastwards.

'James, come wi me, lad, we'll rouse Baillie Cambo.'

The father and his other son ran west. Two baskets of lines lay baited in the middle of the brae, and an empty yawl idled about the harbour in the great shadow of a foreign ship.

By the time David Cambo reached the harbour with the Learmonths, the village snails were straggling down to the shore in a thin ragged line. A gangplank had now been laid down and some men were standing on the quay. One of them was a very big man. He looked more like a statesman than a soldier. He had a grave face, with grizzled hair, and his beard was as white as Learmonth's.

This man made a sweeping bow in the direction of the official and the fishermen as they stepped near. Then, becoming erect, he spread his arms wide and started to speak in a loud, sharp voice. A shower of Spanish phrases tinkled and glittered like foreign coins across the still gold plate of the tide.

David Cambo put his hands up for him to stop. Then he waved with his arms, meaning them to go back on board. To everyone's surprise, the old Spaniard obeyed, signing to his countrymen to do the same.

'Would he understand Latin, do you think?' said the baillie.

'I've sent already for Mr Melville', Learmonth said. 'He'll make him out in Latin, or in any other tongue he cares to babble in.'

Footsteps clattered down the braeside then, and everyone saw James Melville's servant stop halfway down. He shouted to the small crowd.

'They're to come to the Tolbooth right away. Just the commander, and any captains and gentlemen!'

Cambo signalled to the twenty or so men on deck – all the common soldiers and seamen must have been sent below – and they trooped ashore again with slow dignity. Learmonth gazed at the glitter of their clothes, their bronzed cheekbones and deep dark beards, their brown eyes.

'You come wi me, William', Cambo said. 'As an elder you have a right to be there.'

As Learmonth started to follow the party, a hand touched his arm. He turned. A handsome unsmiling face was looking into his, a young face, but with a beard as black as nightfall, and the hair a midnight blue.

'Señor', the man said simply.

He was pointing down at the sandy beach. There Learmonth saw his forgotten yawl, pulled up and moored. Looking back, he noticed that the man's legs were wet, his buckled shoes streaked with mud.

'Don Francisco d'Alvarez', he said.

He gave a slight bow.

'Thank you', Learmonth said, wondering at the contact that was possible without language. He smiled a little smile of surprise. The two fell into step behind the Tolbooth party, the Anstruther skipper and the Spanish captain wordlessly linked. As they did so there was a rustle behind them and the tide turned.

Inside the Tolbooth James Melville sat with the chief men of the town, awaiting the deputation. As he rose to greet them, the old commander made his courtesy again, even lower than before, so that his grey hair swept the floor. Moving forward, he touched Melville's shoe with his right hand. Then he raised himself to speak.

Jan Gomez de Medina could speak no English, but it was clear to everyone that Melville could understand every word he was saying. Before he had come, two years ago, to preach and teach at the kirk of Anster, he had been Professor of Oriental Languages in St Andrews University.

Nodding gravely all through the old commander's harangue, the minister rose at the end and made to reply. Before he could do so, another man stepped forward and interpreted the whole story in the tongue they could all understand. Smiling, the minister allowed him to do so.

They had come, he said, not to give mercy, but to ask it. Their commander, Jan Gomez de Medina, and twenty captains besides, had been wrecked upon the Fair Isle after the defeat of their Armada. Many sank beneath the waves, far from Spain, never to see their homes again. Those who had escaped death wandered in great misery, cold and wetness and hunger, for six or seven weeks, until they were able to reach Orkney. There they had met one of their own ships, *Our Lady of Cavadonga*. In it they had come to this little port, to kiss the hands of Scotland, and to find relief and comfort for themselves if they could; as well as for their poor soldiers, still on board, whose condition was most miserable and pitiful. The commander begged that they be allowed to remain a little time in their port before setting out for Spain, where they hoped to rejoin all their friends.

When the interpreter had finished, the commander sank to one knee and bowed his head, and all the other captains did the same.

Mr Melville then got up and spoke for a very long time.

He reminded Jan Gomez that the Spaniards had no religious or political claim on them, being both Catholics and enemies of England, with whom Scotland was indissolubly leagued. Moreover he was aware that the Spaniards had imprisoned and executed as heretics men of their nation who had fallen into their hands in the past. Nevertheless, he looked on them as fellow creatures suffering great hardships, and he and his fellow townsmen would give them every kind of relief and comfort in their power.

'However', Melville said, 'I have to tell you that you are sorrily mistaken in thinking that yours was the only group of ships to have been wrecked.'

Jan Gomez raised his old eyes to Melville's as the interpreter spoke the words quickly into his ear.

Melville went on.

'The Lord of Armies, who rides upon the wings of the winds, has directed near hand every last one of your hulks and galliots to the islands, rocks and sands, whereon He destined their destruction. And the greater part of your friends He has committed to the great deep.'

At this point the minister took up from the table in front of him a paper. It was, he said, a printed account, which he had bought in St Andrews the previous afternoon, of the number of galleons lost, the names of the chief men who had perished, and the savage treatment the survivors had met with, in England and Ireland, the Highlands and Wales.

The minister then read out every single name.

At the end of it, the old man, still on one knee, put his other knee on the floor, bent his back until his brow touched the ground, covered his face with his hands, and wept. The scalding drops rained down onto the floor in front of him until Learmonth thought they would never cease.

Understanding broke, and the tide of grief flowed through the assembled captains. Nearly every one of them wept. Some buried their heads in their cloaks. Some turned their faces to the wall. But Learmonth noticed that Alvarez stood silent – moved, it seemed, but deep in thought. His eyes met Learmonth's.

Breaking in on their clamour, Melville announced that the commander and his captains, being gentlemen, would be invited to take refreshment at the homes of himself and the magistrates. But the soldiers would have to wait for the authority of the Laird of Anstruther, who would speak for the King. Then they might be allowed to come on shore. In the meantime, kail and fish would be taken on board, and relief would be granted where it was possible.

The captains then went out severally with various men of the town. Baillie Cambo said that he would take Alvarez to his own house. But the Spaniard shook his head smilingly and pointed to Learmonth.

'Yes, let him come wi me', Learmonth said. 'If he wants to enter the house of a poor fisherman, let him come. It'll be all the poorer now for there will be no fish taken this day, I'll be bound.'

'Maybe he'll give you a hand the morn.' Cambo grinned.

Learmonth nodded, and smiled himself. James and Andra had stayed on down at the harbour with all the other young men, eager to take in the glory of *Our Lady of Cavadonga*. Learmonth took the man in the direction of his simple roof. They walked without words but bound by some form of strange understanding. They reached the door, and the old man waved the young one in.

Isobel's voice came from the back.

'Is that you back already, father? What have you brought me today?'

Learmonth went in behind Alvarez. The three stood and looked at one another.

There was a long silence.

In the days that followed, the Spanish sailors came on shore and were allowed many freedoms. They were even allowed to mingle with the unmarried fisher girls, fair complexions flushing at the dark, blue eyes glinting at brown. Some say that the record of such meetings is still to be seen – not in the Public Records Office, but written into the eyes and faces of the children of today.

But no eyes looked longer and deeper into one another than those of Isobel and Alvarez in that first mysterious moment. Alvarez saw before him the fairest flower of all the field. Isobel saw a man tall and terrible, like an army with banners, suddenly kneel to her, subdued. Learmonth, in that moment, watched a great dark tree spread itself out in his cornfield. He sensed the moment spread itself out in time. He waited breathlessly for it to wither. What would happen when *Our Lady of Cavadonga* set sail?

What happened was this.

The Spaniards took a farewell that differed greatly from the manner of their arrival. Nearly three hundred seamen and soldiers lined the sides of the *Lady of Cavadonga* at sunset. They were cheering their heads off. The Anstruther folk stood on the shore waving and shouting as the vessel was towed slowly out of the harbour to await the next wind.

Alvarez had said his farewell. He was bound to take ship, under his commander, back to King and country. Isobel stayed in the house, sewing in silence, with dry, unblinking eyes. Learmonth left her there, his heart like a stone in his chest. As the evening breeze sprang up he watched *Our Lady of Cavadonga* weigh anchor. Her sails fluttered and filled, and his hope for his child dwindled to a speck at sea.

That night there was silence from Isobel's little part of the house. But Learmonth sobbed for his daughter into his pallet, his white whiskers drenched with tears. He knew what she was suffering.

It was the middle of the night when the knock came to the door. The old man had fallen into a sleep heavy with heartache. But Isobel rose from a sleepless pallet, her heart on fire. She unbarred the door and gasped. Against the madness of the stars there was a dripping black form. The salt sea streamed from Alvarez's hair and beard. He moved forward and clasped her.

When he had tried to persuade her to take a husband, Mr Melville had quoted some passages to Isobel. They were so beautiful she had never found a man to match them. She kept remembering them now, and she said them over and over.

'By night on my bed I sought him whom my soul loveth: I sought him but I found him not.

I sleep but my heart waketh: it is the voice of my beloved that knocketh, saying, Open to me, my love, my dove, my undefiled: for my head is filled with dew, and my locks with the drops of the night.

His locks are bushy and black as a raven.

His mouth is most sweet: yea, he is altogether lovely.'

Alvarez understood not a word. But he understood that she was happy. They stood there beneath the stars until the sea that had parted them had run out of Alvarez, soaking Isobel to the skin, so tightly did they embrace. Her nightdress clung to her bones and they tasted sweetness and salt on their tongues.

One month later they were married by Mr Melville.

Alvarez, who had deserted his ship, also forsook his religion, his nobility, his King, country and calling, and all his friends. He also forsook his Spanish tongue, and learned to talk to his wife.

He fished with Learmonth all of the next year, and brought good luck. The fishes came to their lines as if they were charmed. They glittered there like treasure. The family grew richer. The brothers, however, continued to fish on their own.

One day, when they were setting out with the morning sun, old Learmonth's hand started to shake on the tiller. The next day the shaking grew worse. The day after that was a choppy sea and he could not control the boat. The old man's fishing days were over. He had three strokes that year before the one that finished him in the winter. By then he was a white twisted thing that could not speak.

There were days then that Alvarez would not go out fishing. Instead he would take himself to the kirkyard and sit by the large tombstone that he had erected to Learmonth. Whole mornings and afternoons he would sit there, just staring out to sea.

It was then that James and Andra announced their intention to fit out a vessel to trade to the Levant. Alvarez brought out a belt of Spanish gold. Laying it on the table, he said he would go with them. The vessel was bought and they took the sea's road. Isobel watched them with a heavy heart until they were out of sight. Then she walked up to her father's grave and looked at it for a long time in silence.

They anchored off southern Spain on a balmy night in high summer. The moon was full, there was hardly a breeze, and just a gentle lift on the deep.

Andra, sweating in his bunk, could not sleep. He came up quietly on deck to get some air. He was just in time to see Alvarez climbing over the ship's quarter. Andra opened his mouth to shout. As he did so, he saw the moon glittering like a coin in the deep blue velvet of the sea. Then the tide suddenly turned and the coin melted and ran. Something about the scene made him keep quiet.

As he stood there unnoticed, watching, Don Francisco d'Alvarez slid noiselessly into the ocean. The moonlight drenched him as he struck out for the shore. That was the last that was seen of him, the man whom the sea had brought into their lives with so little fuss, and taken him out the same way. Andra told James about it in the morning.

Naturally they wondered. Did a girl await him, somewhere in Spain – or a mother, or a father? Perhaps other things had called unto him, all the things he had so blithely given up at the sight of a fair face. Maybe the moon's golden guitar had played to him that night a melody so strong that he could not resist, plucked from the salt strings of the sea.

But they agreed not to shame Isobel by telling her the truth about her dark deserter.

When they arrived back in Anstruther they found their sister pregnant. So all the tale that was finally told to her was that Captain Alvarez had been lost in a storm in the Bay of Biscay. In time the winter of bereavement melts away, more than the agony of betrayal. And Isobel was free, as she believed, to marry again.

She did get married again, two years later, to a Cellardyke fisherman, a widower with three children of his own. By that time there was a dark-haired little lady running about Isobel's feet, her complexion burnished by old suns of Spain. But there were no children from her second marriage.

In time Isobel had a gravestone put up in the kirkyard, next to her father's. This is how it read.

THIS STONE PUT HERE BY

ISOBEL LEARMONTH

AS A MEMORIAL OF HER SPOUSE

CAPTAIN FRANCISCO D'ALVAREZ

DROWNED OFF NORTHERN SPAIN

22nd JUNE 1590

AND OF HIS AGE TWENTY FOUR

And the accompanying epitaph:

IF A MAN DIE SHALL HE LIVE AGAIN?

ALL THE DAYS OF MINE APPOINTED TIME WILL I WAIT

TILL MY CHANGING SHALL COME

And on summer days she would go up there and sit by the two stones, with her dark-haired child running about between the tombs. She would look into the little girl's brown eyes. Then she would sigh, and leaning on her husband's memorial, she would look out at the sea which had brought him to her and taken him away. And the destinies of men and women would sound sharply in her ears, like the sound of the sea on shingle. And the fates of nations fall away – like the hush of a distant tide.

Selbie: A Feeling of His Business

JAMES SELBIE, gravedigger – that's me.

I've been sexton here sixty years, and I'm getting on for eighty now. I took over the job when I was twenty, from my father. I've never actually taken an exact count, though I could tell you from the records, but I reckon I've put upwards of six thousand people into the ground. That's five times today's population of this village. Just think, I've buried the whole village five times over. That's a lot of digging.

I think that's what has kept me so fit. Most folk imagine there's a thousand jobs they'd rather do before gravedigging. But look at it this way. The kirkyard here is right hard against the sea. It's a cold enough job at times, especially in winter, but as far as I'm concerned I'm breathing the best air to be had on God's earth. I'm out here in the open, in contact with all the elements, and I'm doing a lot of bending and stretching that keeps my joints supple, despite my age. I've never had a sore back in my life.

Look at it another way. I'm more or less my own master. Where and when I dig, especially the last, is not up to me to choose, naturally enough. But having said that, I'm little fashed by the kind of pressures that bother most folk.

For one thing I'm on my own. Nobody breathes down your neck when you're digging a grave, least of all the one you're digging it for. Time and motion men are a bit out of place here, where time and motion don't operate any more.

Another thing is, you don't hear too much grumbling from your fellow workers in other parts of the country. It's a trouble free occupation. The job's much the same wherever you go. You make a hole in the ground, pile in the earth, and put back the turf. What could be more straightforward?

Mind you, it's surprising the lengths some folk will go to just to avoid an hour or two of labour. Two miles east of here you'll find a man in my trade who uses a hexagonal frame, shaped just like a coffin, and not all that much bigger. He just lays it on the earth and digs inside it. He drew me a diagram once to show me how he was saving himself nearly half the digging. He worked it out exactly by geometry. To me that's no way to dig a grave – by geometry, and with your eye on the clock. That's just no way at all.

I read somewhere that in America, I think, they use mechanical gravediggers in some places. The man in charge just touches a button and pulls a lever and watches a load of metal do the rest. To me that's soulless. It's possible, believe me, to dig a grave with feeling, especially if it's for somebody you've known. You can take a pride in it, just as you can if you're building a house. Mind you, pride in building has just about disappeared, but that's no reason not to make a grave well. I'm not an uneducated man. I've read some Shakespeare and I've read *Hamlet*. Hamlet says to his friend Horatio, about the first gravedigger, 'Hath this fellow no feeling of his business that he sings at gravemaking?' And Shakespeare makes Horatio reply, 'Custom hath made it in him a property of easiness.' Well, I think that misses the point. No professional ever dug a grave with a long face. There's absolutely no question of having to get used to it – at least there wasn't with me. But that doesn't mean you can't dig with some dignity.

That's something a machine can't do now. The least one man can do for another is to take some care over the making of his last home. Mechanical gravediggers! Can you imagine? Next they'll be having mechanical ministers to conduct the service.

In a manner of speaking I suppose we've got some of them around as it is. You just have to listen to them reading the order for the burial of the dead. For as many times as I've heard it, that's one of my favourite pieces of reading. I used to enjoy hearing the bits from the Book of Job.

'Man that is born of woman hath but a short time to live and his days are full of sorrow.'

'My days are swifter than a weaver's shuttle and are spent without hope.'

'We brought nothing into this world and it is certain we can carry nothing out.'

Passages like that put life in perspective for you, so that you can see death as not so bad after all, if life's so terrible.

Few things used to be so grand as one of the old style ministers pointing dramatically at the coffin in the open grave and saying that worms would destroy that body. One old stager was fond of quoting from one of the paraphrases.

'The wood shall hear the voice of Spring
and flourish green again,
But man forsakes this earthly scene,
ah! never to return!'

That sort of thing fairly made you take a hard look at your own existence and just think on a bit about the whole human state of affairs.

But not any more. Most of them these days are content with the earth to earth, ashes to ashes, dust to dust part, and even that they get over with as fast as they can, as though it were indecent. Some of them tell me not to bother about coming forward with my spadeful of dirt during that bit of the service – that's where I scatter some earth onto the coffin – and I'm always very disappointed when that happens. I feel I haven't done my job.

In the old days the ministers weren't frightened of dirtying their own hands from my shovel. One man used to grab a fistful of clay as tightly as he could, and hold it up to the mourners before he threw it on to the coffin, shaking it in their faces. Earth to earth. That was one way of showing a man what he really is. But not any more, as I say. Folk just can't look death squarely in the face these days and that's a fact.

I think it all stems from the modern attitude to death. What with folks' hearts being transplanted and life support machines keeping them going long after they ought to have died, folk tend to see death as something unnatural, instead of the most obvious thing in the world. I'll tell you, nothing strikes me as more natural than the fact that one day I'll just be a few shards of bone lying about in the earth somewhere, and after that just kirkyard clay and nothing more.

It's not that I'm not frightened of death. Everybody's frightened of death in one way or another, whether they're religious or not. I don't fancy the actual process of dying, for one thing – the way I've got to go out of the world. There might be nothing in it, of course, like falling asleep after dinner. But you never can tell, there could be pain and prostration, and nobody actually looks forward to that – the indignity and hopelessness of it all.

I'll tell you something else. Old as I am I still don't feel I've had enough of the world. I enjoy my job, whether it's a fine rimy morning in November or a summer's afternoon. I like reading and watching the television and smoking my pipe, having a jug of beer with my friends. Most of all I just enjoy watching the world go by – the boats going backwards and forwards in the Forth, the seasons turning over, the gulls flying about. When I think that all that can still go on without me, then I've got to admit I do feel a sort of rebellion in me, a frenzy that amounts to fear, I suppose.

And there's fear of the unknown. That hardly needs any comment from me, does it? Even a bairn knows that kind of fear, and the older you get, let me tell you, the more of a bairn you grow back into, from that point of view. 'The mind's aye cradled when the grave is near.' Somebody wrote that.

Not that I'm an atheist. Far from it – I don't think I could do the job if I was that. If I thought death was just a kind of bottomless pit into which the generations have been tumbling endlessly since the beginning of time, then I'm sure I'd go off my head. I don't know what happens to the mystery that is me once they sling the rubbish that's left into the kirkyard here, but I do know that a man is more than muscle and bone.

Once, when I was opening up a really old grave, a man came up and looked in at what I was doing. He said he was a lecturer from the university – a geologist, that's what he said he was. I came on some bones that were so old they were badly discoloured and just flaked away like rotten wood when I touched them with the spade.

He said to me, 'The Bible says that these bones will live again. Can you really believe that?'

I said to him, 'Looking at them now, can you really believe that they ever lived in the first place?'

That's the thing, you see. When you're in my job you're coming across human remains all the time, quite naturally – teeth, bones, skulls, they're all over the place. It's very hard to picture flesh on them again, and to remember that muscles once moved them, that they ran about and danced and sang and steered ships and conquered mountains; that they had eyes that looked at the sea, a brain that understood it, a soul that loved it, and lips that spoke about it. All that's very hard to believe, when you're actually looking at a pile of old bones. And yet everybody knows it's true. Frankly I don't find the reverse any more difficult to believe in – that they'll live again, I mean.

From that angle I reckon that my job puts me in a highly privileged position. How many folk these days ever see a real live corpse (for want of a better expression)? The undertaker saves them all the unpleasantness of that side of things. But even he sees a body much as it looked in life. I see further than that, further than any man –

after corruption has done its work and the spirit has gone to God. Between the undertaker and God there's only me. That's quite a field, and believe me it's a big responsibility.

I see them all on their way, you see, and long afterwards as well. Schoolteacher, doctor, provost – they may have better looking headstones than the town drunkard, once he's drunk himself into his grave, but the same grass covers them, and beneath that it's a classless society, let me tell you. Break up the honeycomb and you find one man smells as sweet as another. Pride, arrogance, selfishness, greed – all have an ending in here.

And I'll tell you another thing. There's folk buried side by side in there that would have never as much as given each other the time of day. They would have passed each other in the street. And now they're sleeping partners till the last trump. There's families too, that bitched among themselves good style till there weren't two left to row with one another. And now they're all lying together as peaceful as you like. I've crammed them all in. Sometimes it's been a squeeze and I've had to go down deep and pack them like kippers, cheek by jowel. But never a murmur, you can be sure of that.

It's just as well. If the dead had tongues there would be some buzz would come out of that green hill there, I can tell you. They'd be like bees in a hive. I sometimes imagine what it would be like if the stories of Judgement Day were true – you know, I mean literally true. If they all rose up at once, what a stir there'd be. I can think of some customers here that would stop on their way to Judgement to have a crack, and God and his angels would just have to wait till they'd finished their blether, especially after so long a silence. Their crack would be as long as the crack of doom. But I know it won't really be like that.

I'm reminded of a funny story though.

My father told it to me, about a gravedigger in the last century. Dysart, he came from. He was fond of his tipple and kept a brandy flask in his hip pocket. Gravedigging is thirsty work, sure enough. Anyway, it was a blinding heat this afternoon, and the sweat was being knocked from his brow into the grave he was digging – he was really earning his bread, you might say – so he compensated himself more than usual from his flask. Well, heat and tiredness and drink soon combined to make him sit down in the grave, where he fell asleep right away.

In these days the mail coach used to rattle through Dysart on its way to Cupar, and it so happened that when it passed the kirkyard the guard gave the dead a really rousing blast on his horn. The old sexton, drunk on dreams and brandy wine, woke up and stood there blinking in the half dug grave. In his stupor he was sure he'd heard the last trumpet! And looking round him what did he see? Not a soul but himself. You'd think he might have been glad to be called. But instead he shook his head at what he took to be the poor show put up by his fellow townsmen. And that's what he shouted out, they say. 'Aye, it's a poor showing for Dysart, I can see!'

Whether that one's true or not, I wouldn't like to say. But I'll tell you a story that is true, and it's anything but funny.

The old man who was sexton here before my father told him about a typhoid epidemic that had him working himself down to a shadow. It got so busy at times that bereaved families had to come and do their own digging. The burying ground got to be like a field of giant mole-hills. There were even examples of the doctor telling the sexton not to take the trouble filling up a grave after a burial, because it would be needed again within the week, or even the hour, with members of the same family falling victim to the disease.

Anyway, the bug had only just blown itself out, the weeping and wailing was over, and the whole village practically was walking about wearing black, when somebody reported that an old tinker who lived on the muir outside the town, had caught the tail end of the storm and died. Tinker Johnny, they called him.

Six men took a coffin up to his tent and nailed him down on the spot. Then they hoisted him shoulder high and started off with him to the kirkyard here. That was his funeral procession. There was no minister and no following.

He got a hymn though.

They were only halfway to the kirkyard when one of the men thought he heard a noise. The second time they stopped and listened. Sure enough, there was a kind of groaning, they thought, coming from the inside of the box. They laid it down and looked at each other. Then without a word they picked it right up again and walked on. They didn't want the whole thing starting off again, did they – especially with themselves?

After a time the old tinker actually started knocking on the roof of his coffin. By this time the bearers had reached the front street, where folk were going about their business. So to drown out his cries for help, they struck up one of the paraphrases.

> 'O may the grave become to me
> the bed of peaceful rest,
> Whence I shall gladly rise at length
> and mingle with the blest!'

That's what one of them started to sing, so I'm told, and they all joined in. Raising their voices like a congregation, they bore him to the spot which the old sexton had prepared for him. They lowered him into his grave then, and all seven of them went mad spading in the earth, and him screaming and hammering all the while.

Can you imagine what it must have been like for him, hearing the first clods come thudding onto his coffin lid, and the sound of the spades gradually dying away? Then a darkness and silence that you just can't conceive.

Worse than that, I think, is picturing what it was like for them. How long before the earth muffled up his cries. Would cries like that ever leave you, even in your sleep?

Well, that grave was never marked, but my father was shown the spot and he showed it to me. It's many years past now I had to open it, for it was unclaimed ground, and I'll never forget the sight that met my eyes. It made my blood run cold. These bones were like a Chinese puzzle, all twisted and turned into the most awful pattern that to me was just like the sound picture of a scream, white and terrifying. A scream that had never stopped – it had been going on in the earth all these years. They had a voice, these bones. I smashed the pattern to bits with my spade and the noise in my ears went away. But it was hellish, the worst sight I've seen in my life. And I dream about it to this very day.

That's one of the disadvantages of the job – you see some sad sights, though I'll be bound you'll see sadder ones in some other professions. It's not folks' remains, it's the things they get buried with that bothers me. Wedding rings, for example, or sometimes photographs. They're usually blotted out by the time you get to them, but sometimes you can make them out. What I hate most of all are bairns' toys, dolls and things like that. In fact it's these tiny wee skeletons that bother me the most. I can never get used to them. There are precious few infant burials these days, mind you, but they happen all the same, and the older graves are full of them. What's the point of being born at all, I ask myself, if you're buried within a year? I've never yet heard a decent answer to that one.

Digging up somebody you've known, to make room for a

relative – that's something that puts me neither up nor down as a rule. I do it all the time. But every now and then it kind of gets under my skin. It depends on who it is.

I felt like that when I came across Rob Lumsden, for example, eleven years after I'd put him in. Lord Lumsden they called him – he was the sweep here, and a kinder man you couldn't hope to meet. He had a heart of gold. He'd a fund of funny stories too, and he told more lies than there are hairs on a cat. But the bottle was what made and unmade him. It was great to see him up on a lum, roaring drunk and lurching along the rooftops in all weathers, singing like a lintie. He just didn't care. Maybe that's why they called him Lord Lumsden – that, and his fondness for the drink. It was drink that put him to his grave.

I remember the morning I looked in on him. I'd never seen him with anything but a black face. For some reason the sight of that white skull – not a spot of soot on him – gave me an empty feeling. I just sat down on the edge of his grave and girned. I knew exactly how Hamlet felt when the sexton showed him Yorick's skull. 'To what base uses we may return, Horatio.'

I felt funny too when I came across Peggy Wilson. She was a local beauty, and a real stunner she was too. The men round here would give anything just to walk her along the braes and hold her hand for an hour or two by the kirk wall. I used to see her about here often, and she always took the time to give me a word or two, though I was anything but a youngster myself, even at that time. She was gored to death by the Balcaskie bull, running mad in the muirs – a right bad beast that was – and the young man that was with her was maimed for life trying to save her. She was buried in an early grave, and a damn shame that was. That was nearly fifty years ago.

I had to dig into that ground twenty years back. What a turn it gave me! Her hair used to light up her face like sunlight. And to look at her then! 'To this favour she must come.' It reminds me of another verse.

'Golden lads and girls all must
As chimney-sweepers come to dust.'

That's Shakespeare too, isn't it? Anyway, these are some of the shocks you get.

So it has its ups and downs, this job, just like any other. It has that. What depresses me is reopening the same grave over and over within a short space of time. Normally you go for years before you come back to a lair, though it's not uncommon to have to open one up twice in the same year, because an old man and wife have a habit of dying within months of one another. That's a fairly frequent happening, as a matter of fact. But four or five times is depressing, and yet I've had to do it. The turf is just starting to heal when you have to cut it out in squares and stitch it back again.

Once I'd no sooner filled in a grave after a young woman's funeral, than I heard that her father had gone home and died of the shock of it all. Heart attack. I had to start digging it all up again right away. It's not the work I mind, it's just depressing somehow.

Another time I had to fill up a grave after I'd just dug it, because it turned out the old man it was for wasn't dead after all. They call him 'Cheat-the-Grave'. He got the length of the mortuary and sat up and asked for a cup of tea. Since then he's been on his death-bed times without number, till his family are fair scunnered with him. To make matters worse, he's a Roman Catholic, and the priest in Pittenweem, who just has a bike for transport, has pedalled that journey the same number of times, whatever that is now, to give him the last rites. One time he had a puncture and just turned back, saying that it was a sign, and that by the time he phoned, the old fiend would be well again. And that's the way it turned out, a sort of modern miracle. I heard from somebody that if there's one more false alarm the priest's threatened to send the last rites by telegram! As for me, I'm like doubting Thomas. I'll want to poke him in the ribs a few times, good and hard, before I lift up my spade to turn a foot of earth on his behalf again. He's unkillable. Sometimes you just have to laugh.

A real killer though, and anything but a laugh, is a hard frost, in January or February say, which is my busy time. I know some men that will use an electric drill to break up the first couple of feet. But not me. I don't hold with machinery under any circumstances. Mattock and spade, these are my tools. And a pickaxe if the ground's really hard. One winter I had to get the leeks out of my own garden using a hammer and chisel – there was no other way. That season the frost went on for three months solid without a break and folk were dying at the rate of knots. Digging graves that year was no joke, let me tell you.

Trees can be a pest as well. Their roots spread everywhere, and I've often had to put down the spade and get the saw out. I've seen skeletons looking as if an octopus had got hold of them, roots twisting right through eye-sockets and everything, it's incredible.

I must tell you though, there's one compensation and that's my elderberry trees. These are the trees that line the west wall. I make my own wine from the grapes, and I can tell you I've had some great vintages from them. What else would you expect? They're fed with the best compost you can get, these trees – their toes are right in among the boxes, tapping all the goodness, the very source and mouth of life. I offered the present minister a glass of the stuff and he just couldn't get enough. Then when I told him what it was and where it had come from, he was mortified. Now I can't understand that. All flesh is grass, I told him – he ought to have known that. The whole universe is eating and drinking itself, isn't it? But he thought it was gruesome, my store of elderberry wine, made from mortality and drawn from the cellars of the dead. Chateau La Mort.

I've an elderberry tree in my own garden, and I make wine from that as well. Not with human compost though. I'll tell you what I do. I dig in dead cats wherever I can find them. They're the best. The farmer once gave me a whole sheep, a ruined one. But cats improve the flavour of your fruit no end. I've nothing against cats, I've got one at home myself and we're the best of friends. But after he's dead he'll do me one last service. Why not? Waste not, want not, that's what I say.

If folk find anything wrong in any of that, it just goes to show that what I was saying earlier is true. There's too much squeamishness about death these days, and not enough poetry. Every year, before the fruit forms on these elders, you get the white flowers. On summer nights the fragrance can be really piercing and they're like scented stars hanging just above your head. As if the dead had come out for the night, in another form. That's when I'm always reminded of that bit from Omar Khayyam.

> 'Now the New Year reviving old Desires,
> The thoughtful Soul to Solitude retires,
> Where the White hand of Moses on the Bough
> Puts out, and Jesus from the Ground suspires.'

But people just don't think like that any more.

You can see that from most of the modern day headstones and their epitaphs. They used to take some trouble over a stone in the old days, with the emblems of mortality carved along the top and sides – skull and bones, the sexton's tools, the hour-glass, and the Angel of Death. And usually a grand sounding verse on the back. I know all the old verses here by heart. This one, for example.

'Naked as from the earth we came,
and entered life at first;
Naked we to the earth return,
and mix with kindred dust.
How still and peaceful is the grave!
where, life's vain tumults past,
Th' appointed house, by Heav'n's decree
receives us all at last.'

That one's my favourite, I think.

They didn't have to be so long as that either, these old inscriptions, to be impressive. One of them here just reads, 'Here lies all that *could* die of John Davidson.' Think of the faith that lies behind that one little word, 'could'. You've got to admire it. You don't get faith like that nowadays.

They stopped making stones quite so big in this century, partly for reasons of cost, I suppose, and so the verses got smaller too. Still, up until a while ago they always left room at the bottom for a nice bit from the bible, a consoling sort of text, like 'Until the day break and the shadows flee away', or just 'The morn cometh', something like that. But these days you get something really peely-wally, such as 'Sadly missed' – no religious feeling behind it at all, not even any poetry. That's what I miss most of all, the poetry.

A lot of the stones nowadays have nothing at all on them, just the names and dates of the deceased. Can you imagine anything more dull of soul? There's one stone here that marks the grave of a teenager. He was killed in a motorbike accident in the late fifties. Do you know what his epitaph is? I'll tell you. 'A great Elvis fan.' I ask you! What would that mean to somebody clearing away rubble and dust in a couple of hundred years? What kind of immortality is that? I suppose it's appropriate enough to our age, with its cheap tin gods that don't even last out the age itself. It's as I say, there's no poetry left in death now. It's not just a matter of economics, though there's that to consider. It's the spirit that's missing in addition to the flesh. From the point of view of feeling as well as finance, folk are just no longer giving death his due. That's a fact.

Not Without Honour

IT WAS always the same in St Monans on Sunday mornings, west of the town.

To begin with the sea and the seagulls were the only things that moved – blue whisperings on the shingle and white circlings over the chimney-tops; and webs of sunlight winking on the weed-grown walls of the quiet piers.

After an hour or two the village began to shake itself into wakefulness.

At first it was just the fringes of the tapestry that fluttered and stirred – the old folk who never properly slept at all, and were always up at the crack of dawn. Slippered old wives shuffled across their scrubbed doorsteps, scattering the crumbs of frugal breakfasts over their front dykes, to the sparrows. An old man tottered to the end of the farthest pier, lit up his pipe, and smoked in silence as he stared across the blue stretches of the firth, remembering.

He half turned as the strains of Radio One stabbed into the silence of the morning, breaking out from an open window, over the still harbour.

> Imagine there's no heaven –
> It's easy if you try.
> No hell below us,
> Above us only sky.

He turned back again to his scrutiny of the far horizon and smiled a little smile to himself as he puffed, remembering another religion, a different song.

Soon the chimneys were chanting the age-old songs of the hearth, and the Sunday morning smells of bacon and sausages were curling around the stacked fishboxes and into the meshes of empty lobster-creels, to mingle with the scents of tar and tangle, sunlight and salt.

Down in Gerrard's, the reprobates were buying the *News of the World*, and their kids were loading up with lollipops and bags of caramels, to take back to the fleshpots of their godless sitting-rooms.

But all along the windowed streets the various elect were wending their ways to the appointed places.

The O'Briens, in jeans and headscarves, had already taken the bus to the chapel in Pittenweem, for early morning mass. The Congregationalists, on whom age had snowed white hairs, were toiling up their hill with difficulty, to the Braehead Church. Fawn-overcoated and bowler-hatted, the Open Brethren were making for the Gospel Hall, the Close Brethren for the Meeting Place, Fergusson's Brethren for the Mission, and Duff's Brethren for a leaky shed that wore no frivolous name at all. This morning the Pilgrims, who usually met in each other's houses, were having an open air meeting at the foot of the west wynd. The Sally Ally had formed their ranks in the Army Hall, and soon, with a silver snarling of trumpets, the beauteous files were marching as to war.

The main parade though, was put on by the members of the Old Kirk, at the west end of the town. Under its sea-splashed walls came banker and bankrupt, spinster and strumpet, schoolteacher and fisherman. From all airts they came, in dark flowing tributaries of black and navy blue, amid which the hats of the women bobbed like brightly coloured corks in a stream. Along the nave and into the white arms of the transepts they spread. And the Old Kirk took them all in, under its lichened slates – just as its green graveyard accepted eventually the total spectrum of the town.

Only The Preacher walked alone.

Towards eleven o'clock, old William, whom they called The Preacher, emerged from his cave at the end of the village, a stone's throw from the kirk. This was the original cave of St Monan, so it was said – a deep gash cut into the beetling brow of the braeface, where it frowned onto the sea. William had lived here since he cracked up, three years ago.

Though it was a fine summer's morning, he shambled out in the long black overcoat that he always wore, come rain or shine. From one of its ripped pockets the slanting neck of a bottle caught the sun, spreading it like a star. His white hair stuck out in all directions from his head, like the feathers of a wrecked gull. The long loose ends straggled over his turned up collar. Under his right arm he was carrying a large, battered looking bible. He staggered a little as he turned eastwards into the town.

The first man he saw when he reached the top of the west wynd was James Brand, the provost. His was the very last house in the village, one of a smart row of big bright bungalows, strung out along the braeheads, each one as like its neighbours as imitation pearls, each one commanding a fine high view of the Firth of Forth. Mr Brand's own bungalow was perched near the edge of the brae, its foundations separated by only a few feet of sandy soil from the rocky roof of the hermit's cave. In this way the provost's feet daily trampled William's head, and the old man lived below in a kind of dark age penance.

The provost was just coming out of his sun-porch as William reached his front gate. The two men stopped and looked at one another.

'Are you going to be with the Lord Jesus Christ today, Mr Brand?'

The provost strode down his paving stones between Livingstone daisies and neat little pansies. He was wearing a cream-coloured suit and shoes to match.

'I'll tell you where you're going to be, squire, if this goes on a day longer.'

He jerked a thumb over his shoulder.

'Up at the court in Cupar – where I'll be on the bench.'

William's long leek of a body straightened slightly.

'I'm not breaking the law', he murmured.

'You're disturbing the peace – every bloody Sunday. For that I can have you locked up, no problem. Do you understand? Aye, and I can have you locked away in other places too.'

He nodded narrowly as William's face puckered.

'It's not just Sundays, neither.'

The side door of the house banged shut and Mrs Brand came quickly across the garden, threading her way sharply between trailing stems. She was as thin and bright and joyless as a darning needle. She thrust her pointed jaws into William's white stubbly face.

'We were kept off our sleep last night till all the hours', she shrilled. 'You and your bloody hymns, down there in that godforsaken sty of yours!'

William turned and moved slowly on his way.

'You've not heard the last of this.'

As Mrs Brand's words perforated the hour, the slow sullen chanting of a hymn broke like the turning tide against the flat calm of the morning.

'Holy, holy, holy, Lord God Almighty!
Early in the morning our song shall rise to Thee.'

'See that now, we're late', said the provost to his wife angrily.

And the two of them hurried westwards in the direction of the Old Kirk.

William came to the heavily studded doors of the Congregational Church just as they were reaching the end of their first hymn. The black metal bolts gleamed in the sun against solid oak. He turned the huge handle and stood for a moment in the marbled vestibule, struck by the slanting shafts of sunlight in which the silver dust swirled. He opened the inner door.

White hairs glistened like foam on the sea of heads that swept up to the pulpit. The Reverend Soutar was arranging his papers in front of him. He opened his lips for the Old Testament reading, saw William standing there, a gaunt shadow at the back of the church, and shut his mouth again. The congregation waited.

'I'm preaching at the old saint's pulpit this morning', William announced quietly, 'if anybody wants to come along.'

Mr Soutar stood like a poker in his pulpit and pointed his white finger at William.

'Any man is welcome within these walls', he said sternly. 'Any man that is both sober and decently dressed. But there's no man or woman here is going to leave God's house to follow a drunken scarecrow down to the water.'

'They followed John the Baptist to the water', William said. 'And Christ himself', he added more loudly.

'That's enough of that blasphemous talk', shouted the minister. 'Please leave this place at once.'

William stood for some seconds longer, staring at the blind backs of the heads that no longer bothered to turn round. He turned finally and shuffled on his way.

The sun was dancing in the firth where the seagulls screeched and swung.

When he came to the Gospel Hall, the Open Brethren were benched in a heavy silence of bent heads and deep holy breathings. They were waiting for the spirit to descend and make their members eloquent with tongues of fire. They had been waiting like that for ten minutes.

William broke the sacred vessel of their silence.

'Is any of you going to the true church today?'

The silence closed, like a wound miraculously healed.

'Is there anybody going down to the true church?'

The silence closed again. It was as if a sacred seal had been set on their lips, which only the trumpets of angels might break.

At last Andrew Cargill stood up and turned to face William.

'There's only one true church', he said. 'And that's the church of Jesus Christ.'

His tongue burst into flame.

'And that', he roared, 'is neither to be found in any of the establishments along the road there, where men are accepting a monthly cheque for preaching the gospel – nor down among the rocks from the lips of a sinner.'

'We're all sinners', said William.

'Aye, that's so', Cargill replied, 'but there's sinners and sinners. In this hall there's sinners that are saved, and outside its walls there's sinners that are not saved. And there's the difference.'

He looked at William's poor clothes.

'In your present state there's small doubt which side of the fence you're on. Now away with you man, and don't hinder the word of the Lord any longer.'

As the old man closed the door behind him the spirit crackled in Andrew Cargill and his opening words leapt in William's ears.

'Beware of false prophets, brothers and sisters. For it is written that at the time of the end they shall arise among us and shall deceive many.'

It was the same at the other Brethern meeting places. William was never welcome there either. From behind locked doors his calls to worship were met by closely woven silence. Or sometimes a few words flew out like arrows – quotations from scripture usually, tipped with the poison of fanaticism, feathered with that fatal knowledge of the straight and narrow.

So the old preacher came down the east wynd, as he always did, arriving as usual outside the Army Hall. He stood for a minute, listening to the singing.

> Fight the good fight with all thy might,
> Christ is thy strength and Christ thy right.

He opened the door and stood there, stunned into silence by the glory of their struggle.

The ranks were brave in black and scarlet, and amid the brazen clamour of the bugles the tambourines rang, and their streamers flew like banners, crimson on the fields of sin. Their joy was untouchable. Nor could it touch the old man. He turned without a word and left them to the din of war.

Three minutes later he was at the Old Kirk, a black shadow on its green mound.

He peered inside. The Reverend McClintock was just announcing the offering. As William opened his mouth to speak Mr Brand left his front pew and made for the back of the kirk, a brass collection plate like a shield under his arm. When he saw the old man standing in the open door the smile froze on his face and he speeded up the pious pace he reserved for his church appearances.

William retreated, but the provost followed him right outside the door onto the gravel chips. Clawing at him under the armpit he hissed like an affronted snake.

'Get out of it, you old reprobate – and don't you dare to defile this respectable place with your filthy presence, ever again!'

He hurled the old man from him and the collection plate went flying, its sounding brass clanging among the tombs.

'You're not fit to hear the word of God, let alone preach it!'

Mr Brand's words echoing in his ears, William reeled between the gravestones. The provost then went back into the church. William stood in the sunshine, blinking hard. Then he tottered down the stone steps that went down to the rocks.

He picked his way among boulders and pools till he came to a high craggy rock fifty feet out from the shore. At the top of this he dropped into a circular crater cut into the summit, so that only the upper half of his body was visible. He laid down his bible on the rim of the rock. Placing his hands on either side of it, and facing the town, he began his sermon, his back to the sea.

The Bass Rock and the May Island swam behind him in the gathering heat – weird blue worlds, lost in the haziness of summer. On the Edinburgh side Berwick Law rose like a pyramid. The gannets were diving in the Forth.

'My text this morning is taken from the Book of the Prophet Isaiah, chapter two, verse four:

And he shall judge among the nations, and shall rebuke many people: and they shall beat their swords into ploughshares, and their spears into pruning hooks: nation shall not lift up sword against nation, neither shall they learn war any more.'

William paused, as if to impress a vast unseen congregation. Not a cloud was in the sky.

He looked at the village that swept away from the Old Kirk eastwards, in a broken, curving line. Its houses presented whited walls brightly to the sea, their red-tiled roofs fast asleep under the sun. From the spires and special places within the clutter of dwellings, ancient tunes went up, curling to the sky like the smoke of old libations. The Holy City was on its knees, this one hour of the week.

From the foot of the west wynd one of the Pilgrims lifted up his voice in righteous rage and a flock of seagulls rose in dissent, winging its way westwards, a white raucous constellation. Just past the Old Kirk it burst, and one of the white fragments settled, screaming, near the saint's pulpit, as if waiting for the preacher to resume.

William went on, repeating his text.

'And he shall judge among nations, and shall rebuke many people.

My friends, eleven hundred and fifty years ago, the blesed Saint Monan came to these parts and scattered God's words among us like broken bread. They were the first crumbs of comfort to come our way, these words of peace and love.

He had not lived here many years before there came also to this country men who feared no Christian god and who bore death in the bellies of their ships. When they landed they cut down our saint with axe and sword. Aye, and many another man of God fell by his side. They murdered the holy men of Adrian at Caiplie, and martyred the monks of the May.

Since that time passed there have been wars and rumours of wars, I know. And many are the men of peace that have been cut down in turn – with dagger and bullet and bomb.

But never in the whole history of humankind has there been a time like the present. Let me ask you then: when can you remember a time when such colossal conflicts have been joined, or when men have prepared themselves for such a wholesale holocaust? And when have the peacemakers perished at the rate they fall today? These are the sure signs, let me tell you, of the very last days.'

As the preacher's voice rose louder, the old men of the pier leaned their backs against the sunlit stones, took their pipes out of their mouths and remarked that old William was preaching the end of the world again.

'It's a gey long time in coming', Tam Innes said dryly.

'He's been at it three years now, near hand – every Sabbath', said his brother Robert.

'Still', he sniggered, 'three years in no too far to be out, considering the age of the world, like. I mean, it's even older than old Jock here. It's just a question of how much longer it's going to go on.'

'Which – the world, or the Preacher? Or is it old Jock you're meaning, maybe?'

'Aye, well', Jock Wilson said, 'there's little need to sneer at that poor man. He's had his troubles. And as for the end of the world, it'll come some day – though its coming matters precious little to old men like us.'

They went back to puffing their pipes, their minds rocking to sleep on the quiet cradle of the incoming tide.

'Consider these past twenty years', William roared, working himself up.

'President Kennedy assassinated, and his brother too. And Martin Luther King – he was a man of peace, anyway.

But that's nothing to Northern Ireland – a place where violence breeds like bacteria and peace is blistered by war.

Just look at these last few months, as well. They've shot at President Reagan, and even the Pope. And now President Sadat, gunned down by his own men. That was a savage deed!

Yet all these killings dwindle down into specks of dust compared with the armageddon that awaits us.

Unless we lay down our arms now, and cease this terrible affront to God.'

Two hundred yards away, in the Old Kirk, the Reverend McClintock urged his flock to stay within the fold, and to keep themselves safe from the wicked wolves of this world.

'Above all', he warned, 'stay clear of the pollution of politics.'

He paused a second, and in the whitewashed silence the congregation and its minister could hear old William's words weaving themselves into the wide screechings of the gulls.

Mr McClintock went on.

'There's a man out there – you can all hear him – preaching to birds and fishes, as he does every Sunday, about nuclear disarmament, and using words like "multilateral" and "unilateral".'

A soft sniggering went round the pews.

'I'll tell you this, friends. I've been a minister of the gospel for more than thirty years now, and I've never come across words like that in the scriptures.'

The sniggering grew, broke into a blossoming of hearty laughter and fat contented chuckles.

'And I've never yet found an empty moment in my life that has not been filled for me by some word from scripture.'

Sunlight poured into the church. Missing Mr McClintock, the waters of the Forth waved their golden shadows on its walls.

William gripped lichened rock between his hard old hands, screwed up his eyes against the sun.

'I will shew unto thee the judgement of the great whore that sitteth upon many waters.'

His voice cracked like a dry pitcher as he responded physically to the stronger language of Revelation. He drained his drench to the dregs, throwing the empty bottle into the tide that lapped at the foot of his pulpit.

'That whore, that spreads herself so wide upon the waters of the world, that same whore goes under another name today. She is known to us as the superpowers – as if a grand sounding name could hide her abominations. Superpowers . . . superwhore!

With her the kings of the earth have committed fornication, and the inhabitants of the earth have been made drunk with the wine of her fornication.

Our own land, that fought so hard for independence, has lain down with her and accepted the filth of her embrace. American missile bases now disfigure this country with the scars of their syphilis. We are ridden with death, I tell you, diseased with damnation. And in disarmament lies our only hope and salvation. God will not save a stiff-necked people that is bent on its own destruction.'

Captain Anderson surveyed his shining ranks and urged them to put on the whole armour of God.

'For we wrestle not against flesh and blood, but against principalities, against powers, against the rulers of the darkness of this world, against spiritual wickedness in high places.'

And he commanded them to stand up for Jesus like soldiers of the cross – wearing the breastplate of righteousness, the shield of faith, the helmet of salvation, the sword of the spirit.

'They that live by the sword shall perish by it', proclaimed William.

'Be in the world but not of the world', the Reverend Soutar advised his congregationalists.

'For here we have no continuing city, but seek one that's to come.'

'God made the world, and he saw that it was good', William shouted. 'If it has gone bad on us, then that is the fault of the men that are in it. If politics has polluted the earth then politicians must be made to purify it. Christ the Lord was not afraid of getting his hands dirty. He went in up to the elbows in dirt and in sin. Aye, from crown to toe he was covered in it, and only his blood could wash it off.'

'Be undefiled and separate from sinners', Andrew Cargill said. 'The devil showed Christ the kingdoms of the earth and he wasn't interested. He knew that he would conquer them in his own time.

The kingdoms of this world are become the kingdoms of our Lord, and of his Christ.'

'We have to work for peace on earth', William pleaded, 'work for it as much in the town hall as in the counsels of the United Nations. Our voices must be heard, crying in the wildernesses of this world, where the wickedness of war is woven in sin. That is the work we have to set ourselves to do. And faith without that work is utterly useless.'

'It was by faith', said Mr Soutar, 'and by faith alone that the prophets subdued kingdoms, through faith that they wrought righteousness, obtained promises, stopped the mouths of lions.

Quenched the violence of fire, escaped the edge of the sword, out of weakness were made strong, waxed valiant in fight, turned to flight the armies of the aliens.'

In Gerrard's the queues had gone down and the battlecry from the Army Hall across the road blasted through the open windows.

> Crowns and thrones may perish,
> Kingdoms rise and wane,
> But the Church of Jesus
> Constant will remain.

Their trumpets sang to battle and the red streamers ran like rivers of blood above their heads. They were an army terrible with banners.

The girl assistant turned up Radio One to drown out the din. She changed the programme at once when news of another IRA car bomb in London interrupted the ragings of the Punk Rockers.

'And I heard a voice cry, Babylon the great is fallen, is fallen. She that was clad in purple and scarlet, drunken with the blood of the saints and with the blood of the martyrs of Jesus.

Babylon the Great, the Mother of Harlots and Abominations of the Earth.'

Reaching deep inside his coat William brought out a half bottle. He wrenched off the top, emptying the stream of fire down his neck. His Adam's apple bobbed twice. The empty bottle tumbled into the rising sea, disappearing among boulders and weeds.

'God will judge this country with Soviet missiles!' the old man roared.

'It will be a far cry, let me tell you, from the Viking longships that once flew like javelins across the Forth. Aye, picture a shower of warheads falling like the rain! When God hits us he will hit us hard.

Out of his mouth goeth a sharp sword with which he will smite the nations.'

As he reeled backwards in his pulpit the strains of a hymn floated up from the foot of the west wynd.

> Whoso beset him round
> With dismal stories,
> Do but themselves confound,
> His strength the more is.
> No lion can him fright,
> He'll with a giant fight,
> But he will have a right
> To be a pilgrim.

The men of the pier listened to it quietly. Meanwhile William launched drunkenly into his own hymn.

> Behold! the mountain of the Lord
> In latter days shall rise.

'Tide's well in now', remarked Tam Innes.

'He'll drown yet, one way or the other', Robert Innes laughed softly. 'Either in the hard stuff or at the bottom of the deep blue sea.'

Old Jock rose without any words. He knocked his pipe three times against the harbour wall and walked westwards down the pier.

The Salvationists were still leading the field to victory.

The Congregationalists sang as if their hymn would have no ending:

> This is my story, this is my song,
> Praising my Saviour all the day long.

In the Gospel Hall, where no pretty organ playing ever accompanied the songs of the Lord, the praise came to its tuneless end:

> It is enough: earth's struggles soon shall cease,
> And Jesus call us to heaven's perfect peace.

Jock clambered into *The Dairy Dell*, slipping an oilskin over his guernsey.

Attached to the little yawl by a rope was a lobster trap where Saturday's catches were keeping fresh, their pincers tightly shut by strong elastic bands to keep them from tearing at one another. The visitors would buy them from Jock tomorrow, their holiday pound notes turning to tobacco smoke in the old man's nostrils.

Jock released the trap from the boat, tying it instead to one of the rungs of the iron steps by which he had come down the wall of the pier. He started up the motor and headed for the harbour mouth, steering westwards after that for the old saint's pulpit.

The holy mount was cut off from the shore now by deep water. Jock made a loose mooring on the seaward side and climbed up quickly, carrying his years as lightly as the creels he shot daily in the summer.

William lay in a blind dream. A swell was starting to get up now, so that a light spray came over the side of the rock, wetting his face. He groaned a bit but his eyes stayed shut.

Old Jock sighed to himself. He bent down to the bible which had fallen open alongside its broken trumpeter. It was one these old style family bibles. It contained blank pages for the recording of all the various births, marriages, deaths, that befell the generations as their flesh flourished and fell, withering like the grass to which it was kin. As he picked it up, a single newspaper cutting fell out. It was a snippet from *The Fishing News*. Jock opened it out, and sitting on his hunkers he read again of how William's only son had died at sea with all his crew, their fishing vessel blown to bits by a Second World War mine. An Anstruther boat had snatched at the first words of a frantically held out radio message, like an outstretched hand disappearing into the waves. But it arrived on the scene to find only the gray North Sea separating several spars and boxes. Deepest sympathy for his father in his hour of grief etc.

Jock shook his head. He folded up the cutting again, placing it back in the bible, which he shut with a thud. Then he shook the old man by the shoulder, stepping to the side to let the sun hurt his eyes.

'Come on, William, it's time to be going', Jock said. 'You've stayed too long in the pulpit again, I doubt.'

'It's a long time in coming, Jock', the old man slurred softly.

'What's that, William?'

'Peace'.

The tears brightened and bulged in his faded blue eyes.

'Peace . . . peace . . . peace.' He kept repeating the word, brokenly. Jock lifted him under the arms and heaved him up into a standing position.

'Blessed are the peacemakers!' William shouted the beatitude with a kind of fading desperation.

'Aye', said his supporter, 'if you say so, old friend. All I ken is they're being shot down like flies.'

He wrapped the other man's arms around his neck and lifted him off the top of the rock.

'Now let's get out of here before that sea gets any coarser.'

The Old Kirk was coming out as *The Dairy Dell* purred away from the saint's pulpit, bobbing high and low on the swell. Mr Brand stopped halfway down the steps.

'You go back to the house', he told his wife.

He walked warily down to the water's edge, following the curving patterns of seaweed until he reached the hermit's cave. He stood there, waiting.

Ten yards from the shore Jock pulled on his waders and dragged

William over the side, his shoes trailing first in the salt water, then scraping soggily into the wet shingle of the beach.

'I don't know why you don't let the old bugger drown!'

'He's soaked', Jock panted. 'Can you get his feet dry? I can't leave the boat.'

The provost followed the two men up as far as the mouth of the cave, where William's pathetic life was lived out among rusty cans and old newspapers.

'I'll help him, right enough', Mr Brand bellowed. 'Into the nearest loonie bin, where he rightly belongs. He's a liability to this community, and a disturber of its peace. There's a law against folk that disturb the peace, you ken.'

'You just leave William alone, Mr Brand', Jock said. 'He's the only prophet this place has got.'

He waded back into the water and a minute later *The Dairy Dell* was bobbing back to the west pier. Jock had a quick look at his lobsters then went back to his favourite seat. His two friends had gone home. So had the Pilgrims, and everybody else. The old fisherman sat down with his back to the harbour wall and lit up his pipe.

For the second time that day the words of John Lennon drifted across the silent harbour.

> Imagine there's no heaven . . .

> Imagine there's no countries –
> It isn't hard to do,
> Nothing to kill or die for,
> And no religion too.
> Imagine all the people –
> Living life in peace.

> Imagine there's no heaven . . .

Jock closed his eyes – trying to imagine it. In a little while a smile broke out on his old face.

And soon he was asleep.

The Woman and the Waves

I WOKE UP crying with the seagulls, but my mother rose and left me in the dark. She came back cold and wet, telling me to rise, for my father had gone to sea and there was much to do before he returned.

My father was known as Venus Peter, after the name of his boat. He was a kind man and smelled of salt and sunlight. He carried the sea in his eyes.

When I was older my brother and I helped get my father ready for the sea. While he was still asleep I ran with Alan to the braes for armfuls of grass. In summertime we ran back to the house with them beneath a roof blue with birdsong. In winter the long grasses were like spears of ice and we pulled them with hands that were on fire, our frosted fingers clutching like lobsters.

Mother laid the grasses in layers between the lines that she coiled into the big baskets, separating them so that they would go down smoothly from my father's hands. Later we learned to shell the mussels ourselves so that we could help with the baiting of the lines.

There were many hooks on a line, a thousand on the biggest one. It had to go down fifty fathoms, my father said, among the mermaids.

'Bait each one carefully, lass', he told me, 'putting the hard part on last of all. Do it like that all the way down to the last hook. You never know, there might be a big one waiting on the bottom.'

'A big mermaid?' I asked.

'What would I want with a mermaid?' he laughed. 'A cold bosom and no bum to spank.'

'That's enough of that talk', my grandfather growled from the corner.

My father's blue eyes clouded over and he shook his head.

Grandfather was like an old twist of tobacco with no more softness or fragrance left in him. All day long he sat lip-deep in the black silence of his bible, from which he seldom emerged, except to mend the creels for an hour or two. But he never helped us in the mornings.

'My work', he said, 'is to carry out God's will.'

So Alan and I buried the mussel shells in the earth at our back

144

door, and carried the lines in the scull between us, down to the boat. My mother was thin-breasted, but when she reached the boat she lifted my father to the side, wearing all his heavy gear, so that his feet would be kept dry.

'A fisherman can't go to sea with wet feet', she said. 'If your feet are cold the rest of you is the same.'

Then she would hurry home, wet-legged herself to the hips, and dry herself in front of the fire. There was no breakfast to be had though, until grandfather had read to us out of the big bible that he carried over and laid on the table like a black marble slab.

'They that go down to the sea in ships, that do business in great waters; These see the works of the Lord, and his wonders in the deep.

For he commandeth and raiseth the stormy wind, which lifteth up the waves thereof.

They mount up to the heaven, they go down again to the depths: their soul is melted because of trouble.

They reel to and fro, and stagger like a drunken man, and are at their wit's end.'

My heart bobbed like a cork in my chest as I thought of my father with nothing but a few planks of wood between him and the billowing sea. His longest line reached fifty fathoms under.

'Hush man', said my mother, 'don't tempt providence.'

A squall arose between the old man's eyes, but he returned to the passage he was reading from, his voice rising in hoarse triumph.

'Then they cry unto the Lord in their trouble, and he bringeth them out of their distresses.

He maketh the storm a calm, so that the waves thereof are still.

Then they are glad because they be quiet; so he bringeth them unto their desired haven.'

We ate in silence after that.

Father shot his lines in the early morning.

While he was away I went down with my mother to the mill stream to gather more mussels. During the winter haddock fishing we tore them from their tough threads with shredded fingers. My hands went white beneath the freezing water but came out glowing like a peat fire.

One winter mother grew big-bellied.

Like a still sail, she had a fluttering one morning, then day by day she slowly billowed and filled. The sickness, she said, was not a sweet sickness. It was a sourness, not a burgeoning. But the gathering went on for her, with everything else. Mussel bait was scarce and a cartload cost twenty shillings.

When her time came we were among the mussel beds one sore morning. There was a spitting of rain and a bitter breeze was ruffling the rock pools. As if a fishknife had gone through her she folded up with a shriek. Then she unfurled herself on the edge of the sea and gave birth.

I scooped the bait to one side, so as not to lose it, and placed the blue bundle dripping red, into the scull, covering it with one of mother's ripped petticoats.

I was six years old and I had a sister.

I lifted up the big basket. The thin cry that came from it was lost among the hunger of the seagulls. The mouth was a tiny red wound. I carried it home, mother walking at my side as if through heavy seas. By the time we reached home my sister had wept briefly at being born and turned back again to the darkness.

Grandfather said that there should be a proper funeral but instead my father paid the sexton a shilling when he came home and went with him to the graveyard after dark.

They put her into the ground without a name. There had been no time. The only baptism she had received was the salt spray that the wind had whipped off the sea in the bleak hour of her birth.

'In any case', said my father, 'what's the point of a name when you've never done anything?'

Grandfather said that her life would be hidden with God.

After that she was never spoken of again.

For two years, or maybe three, I went to school.

The dominie's dark, clouded face came between me and the sunlight.

'What is the chief end of man?'

'The chief end of man is to glorify God and to enjoy Him forever.'

'Sir.'

Alan left school when he was nine. I stayed till I was ten. When he was fourteen Alan went with father, and later that year they left the Firth of Forth with the fleet, to cast their nets on the Lammas sea.

I watched them leave from the braes.

The harbour was a swaying forest of masts that suddenly uprooted and began to stream out towards the sun. The oars dripped silver, the sails' red cheeks puffed and blew, and the dark fins of the

Fifies strung themselves out, hung from the skyline like flags. They were bound for Yarmouth and the lure of the herring.

For eight weeks they were gone from home, their hands hauling on hundreds of miles of nets, landing thousands of cran of living silver. They worked in sunsets and dawns and rising moons, and when they slept at all, they said, they were shooting and hauling in their dreams.

When they came home their teeth flashed as they laid gold sovereigns on the table. Every season my father brought me back presents of glass and china. The plates were always ribbed and fluted, like the sand when the tide has gone out. Shepherd lads kissed milkmaids in a leafy world that was rich with blue and bordered by gold. I was to put these away, piece by piece, my father said, beneath the bed, to save up for my wedding.

By the time I was sixteen I had a complete set.

One season, while the men were away, grandfather turned ill.

He lost his appetite and sat for long hours staring out of the deep windows towards the harbour. The sun filtered dimly through the thick, green glass, bathing his white-bearded face, turning it the colour of the sea, so that he was like a ruined old ship in a bottle.

He seemed to soften as he failed. Some of the warmth of his younger days, that my father had told me of, crept back into him as he slept, and when he awoke, he looked at me with a kindness in his face I had never known. He laid his knotted old bark of a hand on mine and smiled.

'How are you feeling today, grandad?' I asked.

His eyes were drawn again to the windows, as if there were some secret behind them.

'Ah, lass, I'm not long for this earth, I doubt.'

But by the time father and Alan came back from Yarmouth, the old man was anchored to a bed of pain which made him lose all knowledge of us. The thing that spiked him to the bed tore screams from him in the night, and what little food he swallowed was thrust back from him in a black tide of sickness. By day he lay in a trembling sweat, his lips quivering, his eyeballs burning, the ball of his nostrils twitching.

In his dreams he raved from scripture, shouting on God for deliverance.

'O my God, I cry in the daytime but thou hearest not.

I am poured out like water, and all my bones are out of joint; my heart is like wax; it is melted in the midst of my bowels.

Be not thou far from me, O Lord: O my strength, haste thee to help me.'

But he lay for another fortnight after that, burning in a fire that nothing would quench.

I rose to his screams one night. My father was already by his side.

'Father! Father!' he shouted, gripping the flapping hand.

The screaming went on.

I stood in the doorway for a moment, watching him as he blotted himself against the wall in the misery of his helplessness. When he turned round his face was twisted like the devil's. I went to him silently and we stood there, two shadows watching the shadow death do its work on my grandfather.

In the morning the shadow had passed. Grandfather's white beard jutted towards the ceiling. His twisted arms hung out over the bed. They were as thin as ropes, as dry as corks.

'Well', said my mother, 'he went ready to meet his maker.'

My father said nothing. He raised his arm and slammed his clenched fist down on grandfather's great bible. Then without a word he suddenly picked it up and walked out of the house with it under his arm. No-one dared to follow him. When he came back the bible was missing but the hurt was still in his face.

'I threw it into the harbour', he said simply.

My mother put her hand to her face.

'He read that thing as if it were a tombstone!' shouted my father. 'And what did it bring him? An animal dies with more dignity than my father died. It goes dumbly, expecting no mercy.'

That was the longest speech I ever heard him make.

Late that afternoon the elders came to our door in a black, vengeful gathering. The chief elder carried grandfather's sodden bible in his arms.

'May you think black burning shame of yourself!' he roared. 'That was an act of dreadful blasphemy. But no more than is to be expected from a man who has never been seen in the kirk for a twelvemonth. The session summons you to answer for it, and offers you your chance to repent.'

Father flashed his anger at them.

'I'll offer you a chance to leave my house without my foot in your holy behind', he said to the chief elder. 'And don't darken my door again with your kirk faces. The old man did all the preaching that was needed for this family.'

Late that night I heard my father praying.

That winter the *Venus* went down, and only one of her crew came ashore, Adam Reid of Pittenweem.

I no longer had a father.

The elders gloated and hung out his death like a banner from the church walls. For his sins he had been plunged into a watery grave along with all those who had the misfortune to follow him. Only one had been spared as a living witness to God's terrible retribution.

Adam Reid told us what happened.

The *Venus*, he said, had been fishing off Kingsbarns, not far from home, when the wind had suddenly backed and blackened into a gale. They were caught so quickly that they had no time to alter sail, and almost at once the waves became their graveyard.

Adam remembered my father's last words.

The seas came over the gunwale, he said, like snow-covered mountains, and the men were up to their waists in a welter of water. Then he saw my father clasping his arms round Alan's white face. He heard him shouting his final sentence before the wind carried it off and the sea entered their mouths.

'Don't be frightened Alan, your father's going with you!'

Then they were buried beneath the waves that became blue again almost as quickly as they had blackened. Even as he sank some floats were wrapped about Adam Reid's neck, and he rose to clutch at a spar and so to reach the shore.

I went down with my mother, now so suddenly a widow, to Anstruther harbour, where we found a farm cart standing waiting to carry any recovered corpses home. A black-shawled old woman was cradling the head of her son in her arms, her voice keening like a seagull on the wind.

We waited and waited.

The tide sighed and stretched and the great brown tangles lifted and turned, then disappeared. But no corpses came to give us that coldest of comforts.

When night came down we put our arms together, mother and I, and walked wearily home.

Then we sat down and looked at one another across the table.

The sea had turned over once and I had lost my father and brother. It was so simple. Yet it was the hardest thing in the world to alter, and to bear.

For two years the tides came and went for us without a purpose.

No folk of our own fared forth on their darkness; no men came back to us on their floods, laden with the sea's bright bounty. We worked for other men, strangers, gathering mussels from the Eden, near St Andrews, mending the torn nets in the months after the herring season.

Time for us was as dry as our needles of bone that flickered in our vacant fingers. Our movements were without music, joyless as the listless seaweeds waving in the surge. The sea became a weariness.

In the winter of my nineteenth year another weariness entered my mother, a weariness that fed on her blood and drew out her life in the long-drawn darkness of an unheard sigh.

Her passage from life to death was almost imperceptible, like the turning of the tide. One quiet whisper, and she had turned from me, slipped into that invisible strand that always separates the sea and sky.

Her last words to me were that I should waste no time in marrying but be wed as quickly as I could.

I chose John Boyter, a Kingsbarns fisherman who held a cord on my mother's coffin. He asked me for my hand as soon as she was buried.

Our banns were cried at Kingsbarns and the wedding flag was hoisted on his boat, the *Olive*. We were married at the manse three Fridays after that. There was a wild surge of drinking and dancing in the big barn.

After midnight the tide of revelry ebbed away, leaving the drinkers cast upon the shores of sleep. The dancers' feet faltered and stilled. We slipped into our new house like two ghosts.

I saw my pieces of china all laid out for me in the corner cupboard, the ones that my father had bought for me, piece by slow piece, at Yarmouth and Lowestoft, by the strength of his hands and the salt strain of his labours on the sea.

The bridal bed had been made up by a woman with milk in her breasts. It lay in the recess like a white calm snowdrift that the slightest touch would sully.

I laid myself down in its coldness and gave up my maidenhead with no mystery. There was neither beauty nor pain. It was as simple as shelling a mussel.

When it was over I lay in the long darkness thinking of my father, still tossing somewhere on the cold green bed of the ocean bottom, hidden by the tumbling coverlets of waves that worried him in whispers. And Alan, bone of his bone, was he still locked in his father's last embrace? Where were they? Without knowing why, I wept into the secret darkness, and for the first time in my life I wondered what my life was.

John took the morning tide on the Monday.

They were fishing for cod that spring, with the great lines, and I never saw him for two weeks. When he returned, dead on his feet, he slept for two days and nights in the box bed, hardly stirring when I moved in beside him.

On the Monday morning the *Olive* went to the other side of the May to look for ling. It was John's turn to stay ashore and take partan bait. He had a bannock and a herring for breakfast and he gave me a cold little kiss with a shyness in it. Then he took out his creels to Caiplie.

When I answered the knock at my door my arms were floury to the elbows. I knew the man standing there. It was Thomas Mathers, a St Monans fisherman. I also knew the look he wore on his face. I had seen it many times before, on the faces of mothers, wives and sisters. It was woven out of the waves.

'I wasn't far from him', he said. 'I saw it happen.'

Looking over his shoulder I saw a horse and cart, and a man standing by. I knew what thing they had brought me.

'What was it that happened?' my mouth asked him.

'He was shooting his very last creel', Thomas Mathers said, 'when I saw him pitched overboard by an invisible hand. I got alongside of him as fast as I could, but by that time there was nothing to be done. It was a bonny morning too – a flat calm on the water. I could see him lying there on the bottom just twelve feet below me, with the creel on top of him.

When I got him up I could see what had happened. The messenger rope had twined itself round one of the buttons of his jacket – you oughtn't to wear sea-waistcoats to the creels – and he was dragged over the side by the weight of the pot. It kept him pinned down there till he was drowned.

I'm very sorry, Mrs Boyter. There was just nothing I could have done in time. It was just one of these things.'

I went outside, stopping a moment before lifting the heavy wetness of the tarpaulin.

His eyes were closed and his expression was white. But the tiredness had gone out of his face. I felt a deep sorrow – he was only eighteen. I reached out my hand and touched his cheek. When I drew my hand away, a tiny particle of flour stayed there, from the bread I had been making for his tea. When I saw this the tears were suddenly torn from me and Thomas Mathers came to comfort me. But it was not John Boyter I was crying for. It was for all men with the sea in their mouths, and all the women who lost them to the waves.

Was this man my husband? That tiny dusting of flour was all he had of me. His breath had barely brushed against mine.

My fragrance remained shut up.

It was Davy Keay who made me open like a flower.

I remembered his coal-black curls and his white flashing teeth from school. But after three years on my father's boat he had left Fife and gone with the Dundee whaling vessels. I could still see him saying his goodbye to Alan.

'I'm bound for Orkney', he said, 'and the Davis straits.'

Then he had pulled my hair and laughed.

I had eaten the bitter bread of widowhood for two years when Davy Keay came back one autumn and saw me sitting among the herring nets. He sat down on the black bundles beside me and put his head on one side.

'How much do you earn for that, my bonny lass?' he asked me.

'Sixpence a day', I said, 'if I work all day at it.'

'That's a long day and a slow sixpence', he said. 'Why do you do it?'

'I've little choice', I told him simply.

'I'll give you a choice', he said. 'Are the men around here too blind to offer you one?'

I looked at him.

He dipped into his deep blue pockets and brought out a handful of foreign gold. The coins burned in his palm like the suns of strange countries. He had been among mermaids and monks and winters and whales such as I had scarcely dreamed of. I had never seen further than the lights of the Lothians across the Forth, like fallen stars at midnight. Now this man was telling me of the secrets that lay behind the horizon's brow, and I was telling him that I would marry him.

We flowed into one another with long fulfilment, he into the quiet harbour of my arms, I into the running tide of his strange coming, a mingling of milk and honey, of sweetness and salt. Above us the stars blew their silver trumpets and no-one heard them on the earth except ourselves.

Davy said he would do one last season at the whales, enough to earn the gold for a boat of his own. Then he would come back for good, to hug the waters of home, he said – and me.

All the way up to Dundee the bare brown fields were stirring in their sleep, under the covering of the sun. The day was golden blue when I watched him board the *Thomas* with James Bowman of Arncroach who had travelled up with us. The two of them shouted and waved to me from the topsail yard as the ship bore out to sea.

I waited a year and a half.

But I never saw Davy again and the *Thomas* never came back to port.

I was down among the mussel beds one fine harvest morning when a hand touched my shoulder. I glanced up. It looked like the ghost of James Bowman. His paleness took the sun out of the morning.

But neither he nor I moved while he told me what there was to tell.

This is what he had to say.

'There was only once between Stromness and Baffin's Bay that we heard the old cry, "All hands shorten sail!" The Atlantic was like a mirror. It was an easy run.

And we took whales like herring. I've never seen anything like it – we thought ourselves as rich as kings. The oil shone in the hold like brandy and the whalebone was stacked like ivory.

We were hardly into September when the winter came in.

It was just like a great white hand that suddenly clenched one day, and there we were in its fist. We asked the captain to steer for the south but it was no good. The ice had shackled us in. The bergs were like white fortresses barring our way.

Then the cold really clamped down on us.

The whole ship was just like an iceberg itself, hewn in the rough shape of a vessel. The water casks were lumps of ice, even our bunks were solid ice, and when we rose in the mornings we had to tear our heads away – the very hairs were frozen into the pillows.

The only fires we knew were the fevers that made us rave, and the vermin that ate like flames into our flesh. There was scurvy and asthma – some of the men just stopped breathing. It was like breathing crushed ice into our lungs, and some of us simply couldn't take any more.

God and I alone know what else there was. Some men's gums became so black that their teeth just fell out. One man died of a wound he'd had ten years ago. It broke out afresh and wouldn't heal. Our oldest harpooner had had a fractured leg in his twenties. It had been knitted for over forty years but it had to be reset. Others just died of cold, and a terrible death that was. There were some of the men suffered convulsions so bad that their knees and chins were locked together when they died and their frozen bodies were as round as mill-wheels.

As often as six times a day the white funeral processions could be seen staggering with their strangely shaped burdens to the nearest hole in the ice. That's how Davy was buried, Mrs Keay. I thought you would like to know that I helped to bury him myself. He died one night in his sleep and he thought he was with you all the time. Believe me, it was a merciful death.

It was on Christmas Day that the ship was lost.

All round us there was the howling of the wind and the grinding of the icebergs. Then there was a terrible screeching sound. I thought it was some terrible monster at first but everybody ran to the side shouting that the ship was stove in. The timbers were splintering under the squeeze of the ice.

Those that could move jumped onto the blocks that were killing us, and they became our last hope. A few of us that could still walk started the long trek to where we hoped there might be some other ships of the fleet.

I don't know, but I don't think anyone made it to a ship but myself. I stayed alive two days and nights on the ice in time to reach the *Norfolk* before she got clear and bore away for home. That was in the middle of February. The fleet had been shut in for over five months.

When I got back to Anster I was reduced from twelve stones to seven. You can see what I'm like. But at least I made it home. I'm sorry for all the rest of the crews, and especially about Davy, Mrs Keay. He was my best friend on board and you were all he thought about out there. He thought about you all the time.'

And for many years after that, all I thought about was the lad that had waved to me from the topsail yard, thought in my dreams about that stilled young heart, lying so many frozen fathoms deep in the Polar seas, the iceberg the only monument that lay upon his grave.

And my own heart grew cold for sorrow.

When I was thirty years old I married an Anstruther skipper called William Brown. He was ten years my senior and a good man, an elder of the kirk. In his house the pages of the bible turned like the quiet waters. He had his own boat. It was called the *Helen*.

To William Brown I bore six children and of these five died in infancy.

We called our first child Helen, after the name of William's boat. Hers was a frail little vessel. She sickened from the day she was born, and died aged three months.

Three years later we had a son. He was named William, after his father. But he never lived to sail with him. He had just taken his first steps at fourteen months when he caught a cold which put him to bed the very day after he had learned to walk. He never got up to walk again. The cold worsened and he coughed his way into an early grave.

Two months before William died, Catherine and Elizabeth came together, two buds on the same stalk. When Catherine was one year old consumption planted its bright red roses on her cheeks and its lilies on her brow. She withered and drooped and we lost her to the earth.

She had been dead two years when Elizabeth had a sister. Grace was just one year and a half when she died. The invisible flames that burned in her head spread unseen to Elizabeth. The sexton had barely replaced the scarred turf on the little one's grave when he had to wound the earth again, for her sister.

William bought a stone and had it erected in the kirkyard, to mark their graves. It had all their names and dates carved on it, and at the bottom a little verse which William had written himself. It read:

> 'These lovely buds so young and fair
> Called hence by early doom
> Just come to show how sweet those flowers
> In Paradise would bloom.'

I never thought to lay any more children in the kirkyard after that.

Six months later David was born, and he grew strong.

But he breasted the years only to sink with his father. He was a lad of twenty by then, and William's hair was like the foam on the sea.

This was how it happened.

It was a fine March morning when the two of them left the house for the last time, and there was nothing in the eye of the weather to warn me that a squall was coming. I just sat down in my chair in one suffocating moment. The salt sea was streaming through my veins and my hair lifted. Quickly I left the house and walked down to the harbour.

Even then all was well in the world of men.

A breathless silence. And the wide white spirallings of seagulls were the only movements on the face of things. Boat and bird wove their woof against the warp of sea and sky, spinning the white wool of surf and cloud.

Then the clouds began to darken.

Suddenly Spring shook the sea's carillon of bells until they were jangled and harsh and out of tune. Rain flicked its wet stinging whiplashes about my face. The wind ripped open the sea, which bled in a white welter, tore the gulls out of their calm orbits and sent them wheeling and heeling off into space. The boats began to turn for home.

One by one they were whipped to the shore.

We stood and watched them, hooded and drawn, a black huddle of seabirds motionless on the rocks. And as each boat came in several figures detached themselves from the group and ran to meet the men, skirts flapping wildly in the wind, shawls fluttering from their heads.

Soon I was left alone, with the single handful of women who were waiting for the *Helen*. We waited and waited, while the sea stampeded like a mad white bull, plunging and roaring.

Then we saw her, and the shout went up.

But even as we shouted we saw the white forest that was flowering round her stem. Over the gunwales it grew, and over the dark figures huddled on board.

Then there was nothing.

The white forest had withered and the figures were somewhere beneath its ruin, tight in the clutch of those unseen roots that wind to the sea's bottom. A long cry went up from the shore.

It was the oldest cry in the world.

The bodies were long in coming to the shore.

When the men called me down to the rocks I knew that it would be for David. I came as they were lifting him from the boat to the pier. The sea slurped out of his pockets and ran from his hair. As they laid him at my feet and I looked at his body dripping there on the stones, I felt a strange peace wash over me. What was there to grieve about? He was one last child to put to his bed. My husband's body was never recovered.

Over my head I pulled the black shawl of years.

But for ten seasons after that, I went with the fisher girls on the path of the herring.

For seven summers I worked in Lerwick, and for three in Stronsay. Then I came down to the Isle of Man. By the end of every autumn I had reached Yarmouth, where my father had fished years and years ago.

That was ten years of cut hands and freezing feet, the gutting troughs by day and a hard cold bed by night. The young girls beside me lay and dreamed of their fisher lads, and marriages in the morning. I reached out my arms to the darkness. There was hunger in my belly and rain in my hair. But I did not know what else to do.

At the end of my tenth season I was seventy.

By then I was nearly blind, and my hands were so crippled I was cutting them oftener than the fish.

I turned again in age to the rocks of my childhood.

I am now a very old woman, knowing only white hairs and a dark roof.

The ashes are quiet in my black grate. The hearth, once the heart of my house, lies withered on its stalk. It no longer warms me with its red beating. The seagulls have deserted my cold chimney.

But that was long ago.

Sometimes I can earn a painful penny mending nets. At other times I gather limpets. If I cannot sell them for fishbait I eat them myself. One lonely meal is as good as another when you reach my age.

Some summers I walk to the silent green breaker of the graveyard. Winter turns it to a white frozen wave. But I am still waiting for the winter that will take me there, to lie beside my children.

Why am I so old?

At nights I dream of those other folk of mine that lie hidden in the sea. There are whelks on their hands and seaweeds in their hair. And the cold green fingers of the waves strum their bones.

Or I hirple down to the pier and look over the harbour wall. I stand there for hours sometimes, thinking of their bonny heads still tossing with the turning tangles, out there somewhere. Some-times I see them.

All I have loved is turned to coral and to kirkyard clay. Ah, the weariness of time and sea! They have taken from me everything I had, and left me an empty old shell. And yet, time and the sea are all I have ever known.

Death, as I approach it, is the wash of waves inside my skull.

The Furies

VOICE PARTS

SETTING: A fishing village in the East Neuk of Fife: or anywhere.
TIME: Nineteen eighty-two: or any other.
CHARACTERS: Gathered together in the name of scandal, a number of old wives, say two: or three.

FIRST VOICE: Aye, there he goes again.

SECOND VOICE: The good-for-nothing.

THIRD VOICE: Robert the Lad.

FIRST VOICE: Away to the whelks again.

SECOND VOICE: Soft in the head.

THIRD VOICE: Never had a proper job all his days.

SECOND VOICE: Never wrought an honest morning.

FIRST VOICE: Since he left the school.

THIRD VOICE: Never broken sweat.

SECOND VOICE: Not a hand's turn.

FIRST VOICE: He should think black burning shame of himself.

SECOND VOICE: The ne'er-do-well.

FIRST VOICE: Kept by his mother all her days.

THIRD VOICE: He's handy for putting the kettle on, she used to say.

SECOND VOICE: Poor old body.

FIRST VOICE: Though she smoked like a lum.

THIRD VOICE: And drank like a fish.

FIRST AND SECOND: The drunken besom that she was!

THIRD VOICE: And nosey too.

159

FIRST VOICE: Nebby as Old Nick.

THIRD VOICE: Had to know the ins and outs.

SECOND VOICE: From back to front.

FIRST VOICE: From top to bottom.

THIRD VOICE: From here to the middle of next week.

SECOND VOICE: Twenty Questions they called her.

FIRST VOICE: Always asking.

THIRD VOICE: Ask! ask the backside off you.

SECOND VOICE: Ask you senseless.

FIRST VOICE: Ask you what you had for breakfast.

THIRD VOICE: Not like him.

SECOND VOICE: The dour devil.

FIRST VOICE: Never speaks.

SECOND VOICE: Never cracks his cheeks.

THIRD VOICE: Never anything but a kirk face.

FIRST VOICE: Never seen the inside of a kirk though.

SECOND VOICE: How could he, wearing clothes like yon?

THIRD VOICE: A bonny sight!

SECOND VOICE: His grandfather's old sea-clothes.

FIRST VOICE: As old's the hills.

THIRD VOICE: As old's the itch.

SECOND VOICE: Never worn anything else.

THIRD VOICE: Nor likely to, neither.

FIRST VOICE: And hair halfway down his back.

THIRD VOICE: What a spectacle!

SECOND VOICE: Look at that beard, too.

THIRD VOICE: Did you ever see such a sight?

FIRST VOICE: Not in all my born days.

SECOND VOICE: No wonder the bairns call him Jesus.

THIRD VOICE: And Santa Claus.

FIRST VOICE: And Moses.

THIRD VOICE: Cry 'Professor' after his back.

FIRST VOICE: He'll like that, though.

SECOND VOICE: Likes to be thought clever.

THIRD VOICE: A bonny chance!

FIRST VOICE: Some folk say he is, though.

THIRD VOICE: Do you hear tell?

SECOND VOICE: He was a dunce at the school, I know that much.

FIRST VOICE: Never had a backside to his breeks.

SECOND VOICE: Couldn't set a pen to paper.

FIRST VOICE: Shirt tail hanging out.

SECOND VOICE: Till the day he left.

FIRST VOICE: Ran at the nose like a burst pipe.

SECOND VOICE: Bubbled at the mouth like a partan.

FIRST VOICE: Jockie Jack taught him how to read, you know.

THIRD VOICE: An ignorant ploughman!

SECOND VOICE: As ignorant as dirt.

FIRST VOICE: Now he's never done reading.

THIRD VOICE: Too busy reading to work.

SECOND VOICE: He's always in the library getting out books.

THIRD VOICE: Ought to be working.

FIRST VOICE: His nose is never out of them.

THIRD VOICE: Trying to be smart.

FIRST VOICE: Books on astronomy.

SECOND VOICE: And history.

FIRST VOICE: And ships.

THIRD VOICE: What slavers!

SECOND VOICE: That's what he paints all the time.

FIRST VOICE: Nothing but ships.

THIRD VOICE: Would you credit it?

FIRST VOICE: And fishing boats.

SECOND VOICE: Does them for all the skippers.

FIRST VOICE: They're well pleased with them too.

THIRD VOICE: Fancy that, now.

FIRST VOICE: I've seen Eck Scott's above the fireplace.

SECOND VOICE: He must have a something then.

THIRD VOICE: It's not for working, though.

FIRST VOICE: On his backside half the day.

THIRD VOICE: Standing dubs gather dirt.

SECOND VOICE: Or up in the woods.

FIRST VOICE: Speaking to flowers.

THIRD VOICE: It's the want of wit.

SECOND VOICE: And in the kirkyard.

FIRST VOICE: Reading the headstones.

SECOND VOICE: Talking to the dead.

THIRD VOICE: It's the lack of sense.

FIRST VOICE: He even digs up bones, they say.

THIRD VOICE: Do you say so?

SECOND VOICE: Has a skull in the house.

FIRST VOICE: On his mantlepiece.

THIRD VOICE: What kind of a man does that?

SECOND VOICE: He ought to be locked away.

FIRST VOICE: Daft as a besom.

SECOND VOICE: Touched as a tattie.

FIRST VOICE: He must be off his head.

THIRD VOICE: He can play the daft laddie, though.

FIRST VOICE: That's how he got out of his National Service.

SECOND VOICE: Do you tell me?

FIRST VOICE: Made out he was a loonie.

SECOND VOICE: Imagine that!

THIRD VOICE: Sat down on the barracks square.

SECOND VOICE: The lazy sod!

FIRST VOICE: Drew a pickle mice on the ground at his feet.

SECOND VOICE: The silly swine!

THIRD VOICE: With a stick of chalk.

SECOND VOICE: Supposed to be a sodger.

FIRST VOICE: Tried to feed them with bread and cheese.

SECOND VOICE: Not so daft as he lets on.

THIRD VOICE: They had him out in a week.

SECOND VOICE: I make no wonder.

FIRST VOICE: There must a screw slack somewhere.

THIRD VOICE: There's a want.

FIRST VOICE: I mean to say.

THIRD VOICE: Goes out at night.

FIRST VOICE: At the dead of night.

THIRD VOICE: With a telescope.

FIRST VOICE: He's supposed to be studying the stars.

SECOND VOICE: How can he see them if it's dark?

FIRST AND THIRD: The ignorant beast!

SECOND VOICE: I know what he's studying all right.

FIRST VOICE: Nancy Meldrum.

SECOND VOICE: Sticks out like a sore thumb.

THIRD VOICE: Sticks out like the town clock.

FIRST VOICE: Down on the rocks.

SECOND VOICE: Plain as the nose on your face.

THIRD VOICE: Looking up at her windows.

SECOND VOICE: An awful carry-on!

THIRD VOICE: And her stripping off.

FIRST VOICE: Bare scud.

THIRD VOICE: Knowing he's there all the time.

FIRST AND THIRD: The brazen hussy!

THIRD VOICE: If only his father had known.

FIRST VOICE: What ongoings!

THIRD VOICE: He'd have been black affronted.

SECOND VOICE: A pity he's dead.

THIRD VOICE: Below the sod.

FIRST VOICE: Driven to the grave.

THIRD VOICE: Before his time.

SECOND VOICE: White-haired with worry.

THIRD VOICE: The poor old soul.

FIRST VOICE: Though he was a mean as a mouse.

SECOND VOICE: As close as a cockle.

THIRD VOICE: As tight as a cod's behind.

SECOND VOICE: He wouldn't give you the droppings of his nose.

THIRD VOICE: The parings of his nails.

FIRST VOICE: The worst word of his guts.

THIRD VOICE: The time of day.

FIRST VOICE: He'd skin a louse for the tallow of it.

THIRD VOICE: He opened his purse and the moths flew out.

SECOND VOICE: You'd think he'd peed on a nettle.

FIRST VOICE: Lost a pound and found a penny.

THIRD VOICE: He was old and cold.

SECOND VOICE: And ill to lie beside.

FIRST VOICE: He was as cold as Old Nick.

THIRD VOICE: As fly as Old Nick.

SECOND VOICE: Told more lies than there are hairs on a cat.

FIRST VOICE: But he was sober.

THIRD VOICE: I know why, right enough.

SECOND VOICE: Slow with his silver.

FIRST VOICE: The narrow-nosed scrooge.

THIRD VOICE: Never touched a drop.

SECOND VOICE: Like drops of blood.

THIRD VOICE: Never took a dram.

FIRST VOICE: Too tight to try it.

SECOND VOICE: Tight as a drum.

FIRST VOICE: Not like the Lad.

SECOND AND THIRD: The drunken beast!

FIRST VOICE: It's his mother he takes it from.

THIRD VOICE: And his grandfather too.

SECOND VOICE: His mother's father.

THIRD VOICE: He was a bad one!

SECOND VOICE: Drank the town dry.

THIRD VOICE: Drank Shields dry.

FIRST VOICE: And Yarmouth too.

THIRD VOICE: Nothing would cure him.

SECOND VOICE: I've taken it all my days, he said.

THIRD VOICE: And I'll take it to my bloody end!

SECOND VOICE: That's what he said.

FIRST VOICE: He did, too.

SECOND VOICE: Came to a bad end.

THIRD VOICE: Served him right.

FIRST VOICE: Fell between the boat and the pier.

SECOND VOICE: Full as a puggie.

FIRST VOICE: Dead drunk.

THIRD VOICE: Dead drowned.

SECOND VOICE: His neck broken.

FIRST VOICE: An ill life, an ill end.

THIRD VOICE: As broken a boat as ever came to land.

SECOND VOICE: It just goes to show you.

FIRST AND THIRD: When drink's in, wit's out.

SECOND VOICE: His lordship there will be the same.

FIRST VOICE: He'll never live to claw a gray head.

THIRD VOICE: Too fond of the drink himself.

SECOND VOICE: Buys it from Janet Fergusson.

FIRST VOICE: An ill-done wretch.

SECOND VOICE: At the off-licence.

THIRD VOICE: Too free with her tongue.

FIRST VOICE: Beer's not good enough for him.

SECOND VOICE: Too free with everything.

FIRST VOICE: It's got to be wine.

THIRD VOICE: Janet Fergusson's.

SECOND VOICE: You know what they say about her.

FIRST VOICE: Do I not!

SECOND VOICE: Likes funny men.

THIRD VOICE: She's no better than she should be.

FIRST VOICE: Like his lordship.

SECOND VOICE: Can't keep the knickers on her.

THIRD VOICE: Can't keep the men off her.

SECOND VOICE: She's as fast as a cat, that one.

FIRST VOICE: Play with her tail.

THIRD VOICE: A wagtail.

FIRST VOICE: A lady of pleasure.

SECOND VOICE: She's as right's my leg.

THIRD VOICE: She's as common as the road to Crail.

FIRST VOICE: As common as a barber's chair.

SECOND VOICE: A warming pan.

THIRD VOICE: A light-skirts.

SECOND VOICE: She's as light as pipe-reek.

THIRD VOICE: She's slack in the hilts.

FIRST VOICE: Keeps to her back and lets out her fore-rooms.

SECOND VOICE: She's neither wife, widow nor maid.

FIRST VOICE: Her! she's dirt.

SECOND AND THIRD: She's a whore!

FIRST VOICE: Bathes in the nude.

THIRD VOICE: With him too, I'll be bound.

FIRST VOICE: At her age.

SECOND VOICE: Mutton dressed as lamb.

FIRST VOICE: She's no chicken for all her cheeping.

THIRD VOICE: Good morning ladies.

FIRST VOICE: Who does she think she is?

THIRD VOICE: As nice as ninepence.

FIRST VOICE: Can't keep her tongue between her teeth.

SECOND VOICE: Ale-sellers shouldn't be tale-tellers.

FIRST VOICE: Always harping on the same string.

SECOND AND THIRD: Men!

FIRST VOICE: They've all been through her.

THIRD VOICE: The whole town's been through her.

SECOND VOICE: From nose to tail.

THIRD VOICE: From stem to stern.

FIRST VOICE: From arse to elbow.

SECOND VOICE: From backside to breakfast time.

THIRD VOICE: And goes to the kirk too.

SECOND VOICE: A seller of drink.

THIRD VOICE: Sucking in with the minister.

SECOND VOICE: A dealer in dirt.

THIRD VOICE: Giving him the glad eye.

SECOND VOICE: And always has foul fingers.

THIRD VOICE: He ought to tell her.

FIRST AND SECOND: The shameless lummer!

THIRD VOICE: The last man would have let her have it.

FIRST VOICE: He'd have gone through her all right.

SECOND VOICE: Right from the pulpit.

FIRST VOICE: Like a dose of salts.

THIRD VOICE: He wouldn't have missed her and hit the wall.

FIRST VOICE: Not this man.

SECOND VOICE: More's the pity.

THIRD VOICE: His wind shakes no corn.

SECOND VOICE: He's frightened of the day he never saw.

THIRD VOICE: The jessie!

FIRST VOICE: I'd like to spit in her eye.

SECOND VOICE: Batter her black and blue.

THIRD VOICE: Rattle her jaws.

SECOND VOICE: Dad her small as meal.

FIRST VOICE: Dance east and west on her.

THIRD VOICE: Let her feel the weight of my arm.

SECOND VOICE: My foot in her arse.

FIRST VOICE: That's what she's needing.

THIRD VOICE: Her and her five pound notes.

SECOND VOICE: In the collection plate.

FIRST VOICE: Every Sunday.

SECOND VOICE: Her ill-gotten gains.

FIRST VOICE: It's small notice he takes of us.

SECOND VOICE: Our widows' mites.

THIRD VOICE: Not good enough for him.

SECOND VOICE: It just goes to show you.

FIRST VOICE: Poor folk are soon pissed on.

THIRD VOICE: As poor as Job.

SECOND VOICE: The patience of Job.

THIRD VOICE: It's small thanks she'll get from the Lad.

FIRST VOICE: Robert the Lad!

THIRD VOICE: Never had two pennies to rub together.

SECOND VOICE: He knows what side his bread's buttered on.

THIRD VOICE: Never had a nail to claw his arse.

SECOND VOICE: He knows how many beans make five.

FIRST VOICE: He'll spend her money for her.

THIRD VOICE: Make it disappear.

SECOND VOICE: Like snow off a dyke.

FIRST VOICE: And her drink too.

THIRD VOICE: Like it was out of fashion.

SECOND VOICE: She'll have to live on hope with him.

FIRST VOICE: A slim diet.

SECOND VOICE: Make the best of her ill bargain.

THIRD VOICE: The ill-done brute.

SECOND VOICE: The bold boy.

FIRST VOICE: In there every night.

SECOND VOICE: The cock of the midden.

THIRD VOICE: Bending his elbow.

SECOND VOICE: Blearing his eyes.

FIRST VOICE: Having a good skinful.

SECOND VOICE: Carrying some cargo.

THIRD VOICE: Chucking it down his neck.

SECOND VOICE: Downing it like water.

FIRST VOICE: Sucking it in like mother's milk.

THIRD VOICE: Peeing it out at the pier head.

FIRST VOICE: Making himself mortal.

THIRD VOICE: As drunk as a lord.

SECOND VOICE: As full as a gun.

FIRST VOICE: As merry as a monarch.

THIRD VOICE: As tight as a tinker.

FIRST VOICE: Thinks he's awful smart.

SECOND VOICE: Yon's awful doings.

FIRST VOICE: Biding there all night.

THIRD VOICE: With Lady Muck.

FIRST VOICE: Bold as brass.

THIRD VOICE: Winding her up.

FIRST VOICE: Bedding her down.

SECOND VOICE: Turning her like a handle.

THIRD VOICE: Steering her like the wind.

FIRST VOICE: Buzzing off in the morning.

SECOND VOICE: Like a blue-arsed fly.

THIRD VOICE: Like a cat with two tails.

FIRST VOICE: Leaving his washing.

SECOND VOICE: His dirty old duds.

THIRD VOICE: For her to hang up.

FIRST VOICE: Have you seen the state of it?

SECOND VOICE: Gad sakes!

FIRST VOICE: Supposed to be clean.

THIRD VOICE: As black as the ace of spades.

SECOND VOICE: As black as the ash-hole

FIRST VOICE: Washed in the pot and dried in the lum.

THIRD VOICE: He ought to throw out his own fish-guts.

SECOND VOICE: To his own sea-maws.

THIRD VOICE: Instead of leaving it to her.

FIRST AND SECOND: The dirty beast!

THIRD VOICE: The brass-necked besom!

FIRST VOICE: The bad bugger!

SECOND AND THIRD: The shameless slut!

FIRST VOICE: The swine!

SECOND VOICE: The madam!

THIRD VOICE: The whoremaster!

FIRST AND SECOND: The Jezebel!

THIRD VOICE: Look out, here they come now.

FIRST VOICE: The two of them.

SECOND VOICE: Like peas in a pod.

THIRD VOICE: Like semmit and drawers.

FIRST VOICE: Hello there, Robert.

SECOND VOICE: Fine morning, Miss Fergusson.

FIRST VOICE: Fancy seeing you just now.

SECOND VOICE: We were just speaking about you.

THIRD VOICE: Just mentioned your names there.

SECOND VOICE: Just in passing, like.

THIRD VOICE: It's a small world we live in.

FIRST, SECOND AND THIRD: Isn't it just!